CALM IS A SKILL

CALM
— IS A —
SKILL

Calm Isn't a Personality—
It's a Nervous System Skill

By Melinda Charlesworth

ISBN: 978-0-9870479-7-7

For Marcus, Delta, Wilson,
and Mike—my greatest teachers in
love, laughter, trust, and calm.

TABLE OF CONTENTS

CHAPTER 1

THE MYTH OF "NATURALLY CALM PEOPLE"

Some people seem calm the way other people seem tall. Like it's just what they got handed.

They don't rush. They don't snap. They don't spiral. They don't look like they're doing mental gymnastics just to answer a basic question without crying.

Meanwhile, you can be functioning perfectly on the outside, ticking boxes, being responsible, showing up, doing the thing . . . and inside it feels like you're carrying a live electrical wire.

And if you're honest, you've probably had the thought at least once: *Why is calm so easy for everyone else?*

That thought is one of the quietest sources of shame I see in capable people. Not shame about failing publicly. Shame about struggling privately. Shame about the fact that you can run a meeting, raise kids, manage deadlines, hold everyone else together, and still feel as if you can't manage your own internal world.

So let's start here, before we do anything else.

The idea of "naturally calm people" is mostly a myth.

Not because some people don't look calm. They do. But what we're usually seeing is not a personality trait. It's capacity. It's support. It's nervous system conditioning. It's skills that were learned so early they now look like temperament. It's also context.

You only ever see the surface, and the surface can be convincing. You don't see what someone's body does at 2 a.m., how much effort it takes to keep their voice steady, or what happens after they close the door. You don't know their sleep quality, their stress load, their hormones, their support, their history, or what their nervous system is doing behind the scenes.

There's a difference between performing calm and having the *capacity* for calm. People perform calm all the time. They smile. They keep their voice even. They push through. They stay polite. They look fine.

Then they get in the car, and their chest tightens. Or they get home and collapse. Or they lie awake with their mind doing laps, replaying every conversation like it's an emergency broadcast.

That is not calm. That is holding.

This book is not here to teach you how to look calm. It's here to help you become calmer on the inside in a way that's biologically realistic and actually sustainable. Because calm is not something you either have or don't have.

Calm is a skill.

And skills can be learned.

Part 1: The Calm Myth and the Cost of Believing It

The myth goes like this: Some people are just wired to handle life. They're naturally grounded. Naturally steady. Naturally unbothered.

And if you're not one of those people, then you must be too sensitive, too anxious, too reactive, too intense. You must be the kind of person who "overthinks," "takes things personally," or "can't regulate."

It's a neat story. It's also a cruel one because it creates a false conclusion: *This is just who I am.*

Once that conclusion sets in, most people stop learning. They don't stop trying, exactly. They keep trying to cope. They try harder. They push more. They read another book, download another app, tell themselves to be grateful, go for more walks, do more yoga, drink more water, journal more, meditate more.

But underneath the effort is often a quiet belief that they are the problem. And when a strategy doesn't work, they don't blame the strategy. They blame themselves.

I want to dismantle that belief early because it's not only inaccurate but also exhausting. It makes you compare your inside to other people's outside. It makes you interpret stress as weakness. It makes you treat normal nervous system responses like personal failures.

Meanwhile, your nervous system is doing something much simpler. It's responding to load.

It's responding to threat, whether the threat is real and immediate or subtle and relational. It's responding to uncertainty, pressure, sleep deprivation, sensory overload, unresolved tension, constant decision-making, and the invisible demand of being "on" all the time.

This is what I mean by the invisible load. It's not just what you do. It's what your system carries while you do it.

Let me show you how this looks in real life.

Jason gets an email from his manager with the subject line: "Quick chat?"

There's no context. No softening. No details. His stomach drops, and his mind starts racing before he's even opened it. He can feel it in his body first: a tightening in the chest, a quickening pulse, a slight bracing through the shoulders as if he's about to be hit.

Within seconds, his brain starts doing what human brains do in uncertain situations. It fills in the blanks. It runs scenarios. It searches his recent work for mistakes, reads yesterday's meeting through a threat filter, and tries to prepare him for the worst. By the time he sits down for the meeting, he's already lived through an imaginary disaster.

The confusing part? Jason isn't irrational. He's competent. He's not fragile. He's just walking into that moment with a nervous system that has learned, through experience, that ambiguity plus authority can equal danger. The reaction isn't about the email itself. It's about what his threat system predicts could follow.

Hannah is at the supermarket, and her four-year-old melts down because she said no to a dinosaur-shaped cookie.

People are watching. She's already tired. Her brain has been doing logistics all day. Her system is running on a thin buffer. When the meltdown hits, heat rises in her chest, and her attention narrows. She can feel her jaw clench before she even speaks.

Part of her wants to soothe her child. Part of her wants to get out of the aisle as quickly as possible. Another part of her feels exposed, like she's being evaluated by strangers. That's often the hidden ingredient in public parenting moments: a social threat layer. Not danger in a dramatic sense, but the nervous system's old fear of judgment and exclusion.

So she snaps harder than she intended, and then she hates herself for snapping. Later, in the car, she can think clearly again, and she feels sick with regret. But in the moment, her brain wasn't prioritizing wisdom. It was prioritizing containment. Her body treated that chaos as "urgent," and urgency is the language of the Caveman.

Lena's partner comes home quiet and goes straight into another room.

It's small on paper. Nothing has happened yet. But her nervous system reads distance and turns it into danger. Her body tightens, her stomach drops, and she feels a flash of panic that doesn't match the moment. She can almost feel herself bracing for impact.

Her mind moves quickly to meaning. *Did I do something wrong? Are they angry? Is something about to change? Is this the start of disconnection?* She tries to act normal, but her attention keeps tracking the silence like a threat signal. When she walks into the room, she's already primed for a fight or a collapse, even though she hasn't asked a single question.

This is how relational threat works. The nervous system cares deeply about connection because, historically, connection meant safety. If Lena learned early that distance can precede criticism, withdrawal, or abandonment, her body will respond to distance as if it is the beginning of something painful. It isn't drama. It's pattern recognition.

In each of those moments, the person involved isn't lacking character. They're in a state.

Their body is reacting before their mind has even formed an opinion. That is not weakness. That is nervous system biology.

Your brain and body are constantly predicting what happens next. They use cues such as tone, expression, uncertainty, exclusion, conflict, delay, and ambiguity to decide whether you are safe. They also use internal cues: hunger, fatigue, pain, caffeine, hormones, and the general level of stress already in the system. When those cues add up, your capacity drops.

This is why calm isn't "just a mindset." Mindset matters, but it comes online properly when the nervous system is in a workable range. When you're flooded, your body prioritizes protection. The part of you that thinks clearly and holds perspective doesn't disappear because you're being dramatic. It becomes less accessible because that's what the brain does under threat.

So when you look at someone who seems "naturally calm," what you're often looking at is not a better person. You're looking at someone whose nervous system has more buffer in that moment.

Sometimes that buffer comes from obvious things: sleep, support, fewer responsibilities, more time. Sometimes it comes from early life learning. They grew up with steadiness, emotional safety, and predictable repair, so their system learned that stress rises and falls without catastrophe. But sometimes they look calm because they're shut down, disconnected, or numb.

The point is: You can't tell from the outside.

But the myth makes you think you can, and then it makes you judge yourself against something you don't fully understand.

Here's the reframe I want you to carry into the rest of this book:

Calm is not a personality trait. Calm is capacity plus skills.

Capacity can be built. Skills can be developed. Baseline can change.

And if calm has been hard for you, it doesn't mean you're defective. It usually means you've been carrying more than your nervous system was designed to carry without support, and no one ever taught you the mechanics of how to come back.

Part 2: The Invisible Load – Why Calm Gets Harder the More You Carry

Here's something most people never factor in when they judge themselves: Calm is not only about what happens to you. It's also about what your system is carrying when it happens.

Two people can face the same situation and respond in completely different ways, simply because one has more buffer. One has slept. One has eaten. One has had a quiet hour. One has been supported. One is walking into the moment with more capacity in the tank.

This is what I mean by the invisible load: It's the accumulation of demand that does not always look dramatic, but it changes how your nervous system responds to everything.

Some of that load is practical. It's the mental tabs you keep open all day. The logistics. The planning. The remembering. The little decisions that never stop. The constant switching between roles. You might be writing an email while thinking about dinner, remembering you need to pay a bill, tracking a conversation you have to have later, and trying not to forget the thing you promised last week. None of that looks like danger, but it is still load.

There's another kind of load that's easy to underestimate because it looks so normal: the constant stream of micro-decisions. Not the big life choices, the small ones that never stop. What to respond to first, what tone to use, whether to push back or stay quiet, how to phrase something so it lands well, how to keep three moving parts in your head while you switch tasks.

That kind of decision-making relies heavily on the prefrontal cortex, the part of the brain involved in planning, inhibition, and working memory. It's a brilliant system, but it isn't infinite. When it's been running hard all day, especially on poor sleep or high stress, your threshold drops. Things that would normally feel manageable start to feel harder because the cognitive resources that support choice and perspective are running low.

Some of that load is relational. It's the emotional labor of being the stable one. It's the effort of monitoring other people's moods. It's the quiet work of keeping connection steady, especially if you learned early that connection can be unpredictable. It's the tension of avoiding conflict. It's the way you brace around certain people. It's the rehearsing, the second-guessing, the self-editing that happens when you're trying to be acceptable.

Some of that load is sensory. Noise. Screens. Notifications. Interruptions. Background information your brain has to process all day. The nervous system doesn't experience modern life as "normal." It experiences it as a stream of inputs that it must continually evaluate. Your brain is constantly filtering, orienting, switching attention, and scanning for what matters. That is effort, even if you are sitting still.

And some of that load is biological. Sleep debt. Low blood sugar. Dehydration. Caffeine. Hormonal shifts. Pain. Inflammation. Lack of movement. These are not minor details. They change your threshold. When the body is depleted, your tolerance narrows. You have less space between stimulus and response; that is typical of children and adolescents, but in your case, it's because your brain is doing resource management.

In neuroscience, there's a way of describing what happens when the load stays high for too long. The brain and body have a stress system designed to help you meet challenges and respond to threats. It mobilizes energy, sharpens focus, and gets you ready to act. That system is meant to turn on, do its job, and then turn off.

When it turns on too often without sufficient recovery, the body starts to pay a price. Researchers call this allostatic load. It's the wear and tear of repeated activation. In plain language, it's what happens when your system is asked to cope as if everything is urgent, all the time.

One way allostatic load shows up is that your baseline rises. Your nervous system starts living in a higher gear. It takes less to tip you into a stress response because you're already running with the engine revving. You may notice you're more reactive, more emotional, less patient, or more anxious than usual. You may also notice the opposite: numbness, fog, shutdown. Either way, it's a sign that your nervous system has been carrying too much for too long.

This is why you can have a week where you feel grounded and capable, and then another week where one small thing tips you into tears, rage, withdrawal, or panic. You did not suddenly lose your coping skills. Your buffer was smaller. Your system was closer to the edge.

It's also why "just cope better" is such an unhelpful instruction. It assumes the problem is attitude. Often, the problem is load.

If you've been pushing through for months, carrying too much alone, living in constant urgency, then calm is not something you can simply think your way into. Your nervous system needs recovery and support because biology always wins. You can override it for a while, but eventually the body collects the debt.

This is where people get stuck. They feel the strain and assume it means something about their character. They interpret depletion as weakness. They judge themselves for not handling things the way they used to.

But the nervous system is not making a moral statement. It is reporting capacity.

When you start to see calm through that lens, it becomes much easier to work with. You stop asking, "Why can't I handle this?" and start asking, "What is my load right now, and what would increase my buffer?"

Sometimes, increasing the buffer looks like sleep. Sometimes it looks like food. Sometimes it looks like less stimulation. Sometimes it looks like saying no earlier. Sometimes it looks like reducing decisions. Sometimes it looks like having a hard conversation rather than carrying the tension for weeks. Sometimes it looks like asking for help.

None of those are glamorous. They won't always fit neatly into your day. But they are the strategies your nervous system actually responds to because they speak the language of capacity.

And once you start building buffer intentionally, something shifts. The same life events still happen, but you meet them from a different baseline. You have more range. More choice. More access to the part of you that can think, reflect, and respond.

That is where calm starts to become real.

Part 3: Performing Calm vs. Having Capacity – Why Looking Fine Can Be a Form of Bracing

A lot of people assume they're not calm because they don't look calm.

They imagine calm as a kind of smoothness. The person who never seems flustered. The person who always has the right words. The person who stays steady in the meeting, stays patient with the kids, stays measured in conflict, stays organized under pressure.

And to be fair, some people do have more capacity. Some people have more buffer. Some people learned steadiness early and carry it in their bodies the way others carry confidence.

But there's another truth that's easy to miss: Many people who look calm are not calm.

They are contained. They are braced. They are holding themselves together. From the outside, it looks like competence. It looks like composure. It looks like maturity. From the inside, it can feel like running a marathon while smiling politely.

This is one of the main reasons the calm myth hurts. It makes you compare your inside to someone else's surface. You see their steady face and assume their nervous system must be steady too. You don't see what happens after the conversation, or later that night, or in the quiet moments when the body finally stops performing.

Performing calm is a survival strategy for many people. It develops in environments where being emotional is not safe, not welcome, or not allowed. It develops when you learn early that you need to be "easy" to keep connection. It develops when you have to keep functioning no matter how you feel, because the demands don't pause for your nervous system.

You learn to smile while you're anxious. You learn to push through when you're exhausted. You learn to keep talking in conflict even when your throat tightens, and your mind goes blank. You learn to say, "It's fine," while your body is buzzing with stress chemistry.

And often it works. You can get through a lot of life that way. But the cost shows up somewhere.

It shows up in the way you crash after being "on"; in the way your sleep is light and restless even when you're tired; in the way you replay conversations in your head as if you're still in them; in the way you can't fully relax, even when nothing is wrong. It can show up as resentment, irritability, numbness, headaches, gut issues, or that wired-and-tired feeling that becomes your normal.

In nervous system terms, performing calm is often either high control or shutdown. It can be a system that stays activated but tightly managed, where the body is tense and vigilant while the face looks fine. Or it can be a system that goes flat to cope, where you function but feel disconnected from yourself. Neither of those is true regulation. They're strategies. Often adaptive. Sometimes necessary. But not the calm most people are actually longing for.

Having capacity feels different.

Capacity is not the absence of emotion. It's the ability to feel emotion without being hijacked by it. It's being able to stay connected to yourself while pressure moves through. It's having enough nervous system range to be able to respond rather than react, pause rather than power through, and repair rather than spiral.

It's also the ability to be honest without collapsing. To hold a boundary without going cold. To tolerate someone else's disappointment without abandoning yourself. To make a mistake without punishing yourself for days.

That is not performance. That is inner safety.

And here's the good news. Capacity is not reserved for people who were lucky enough to learn it early. Capacity is built.

It's built through recovery and buffer. It's built through learning what your system needs when it's in a higher gear. It's built through understanding what happens under stress and practicing the skills that bring you back. It's built through patterns of repair, so relationships feel safer over time. It's built through repetition because nervous systems learn through experience.

This is why we are not aiming for "looking calm." We're aiming for something far more useful: being able to stay present inside your own life.

As you go through the rest of the book, you'll start to notice the difference in your own body. You'll notice when you're bracing. You'll notice when you're forcing yourself through. You'll notice when you're smiling but tight. You'll notice when you're coping by disconnecting.

None of that is a reason to judge yourself. It's simply information.

Because once you can tell the difference between performance and capacity, you stop chasing the wrong kind of calm. You start building the kind that actually changes how it feels to be you.

Part 4: Calm Is a Skill – What Changes When You Stop Making It Personal

If calm were a personality trait, there wouldn't be much point in reading the rest of this book.

You'd either be one of the people who "have it," or you wouldn't. The best you could do would be to manage the fallout and hope life gets easier.

But calm is not fixed, and it's not fate.

Calm is a skill because the nervous system is designed to learn. It learns through repetition and experience. It learns what to brace for, what to avoid, what to anticipate, and what to trust. It learns what keeps you safe, what keeps you connected, and what helps you survive the day.

This is important because it explains why your reactions can feel so automatic. Your nervous system is not consulting a committee. It is running pattern recognition. It is predicting what happens next based on what has happened before, and then it prepares you accordingly. It makes sense of cues faster than your conscious mind can catch up.

That is not you being dramatic. That is your brain doing its job.

In neuroscience terms, threat processing prioritizes speed over nuance. Stress chemistry mobilizes energy, attention narrows, and resources shift toward fast, protective responses. The parts of the brain involved in reflection and perspective become less accessible. You don't lose intelligence. You lose range.

This is why it can feel impossible to "think your way out" of a heightened state. It's not a motivation problem. It's state-dependent access. What you can access depends on the gear your nervous system is in.

Once you understand that, you stop arguing with yourself.

You stop asking, "Why can't I just be calm?" and you start asking a better question: "What does my system need in this state?"

That shift alone changes a lot because it moves you out of self-attack and into skill-building. Instead of treating your reactions as proof that something is wrong with you, you start treating them as information about what your nervous system has learned.

Here's the most hopeful part: If your system has learned certain patterns, it can learn new ones.

If it has learned to push through exhaustion until collapse, it can learn to respond earlier. If it has learned to ignore early signs until it has to escalate, it can learn that a small signal will be met. If it has learned that conflict means disconnection, it can learn repair. If it has learned that needs are dangerous, it can learn that needs can be named safely. If it has learned that you have to stay vigilant to stay safe, it can learn that you have choices.

This is not about "fixing yourself." It's about updating learning.

And learning updates through evidence.

Not the evidence of a great insight you had once, or a quote you saved, or a promise you made at 2 a.m. Nervous systems don't change because you agree with an idea. They change because you repeatedly show your system something different in real life.

That might look like pausing before you fire off the message. Eating before you become reactive. Taking one minute to settle your body before you try to solve the whole problem. Stepping away from a conversation before you say something you regret. Coming back for yourself after a hard moment instead of punishing yourself for it.

Those are tiny decisions. They don't look like transformation from the outside. But inside, they are the building blocks of trust.

Trust is not a concept your nervous system holds in the abstract. It's a prediction it makes based on what tends to happen. When you become someone who responds to activation with support instead of criticism, your nervous system begins to expect support. Over time, it stops escalating as quickly because it doesn't have to shout to be noticed.

That's how calm becomes possible.

You don't become a different person, but you become more predictable to your own body.

Closing: The Permission Slip

If calm has felt hard for you, it does not mean you're broken, or weak, or failing at life. Most of the time, it means your nervous system has been carrying more load than it has capacity for, and it has been doing what nervous systems do under strain. It has been protecting you the best way it knows how.

The invisible load matters. The difference between performing calm and having capacity matters. And understanding that calm is a skill matters because it changes the story you tell about yourself. It shifts the question from "What is wrong with me?" to "What is happening in my system, and what would help right now?"

That question is not self-indulgent. It's practical. It's neuroscience-aligned. It recognizes that stress is not only a mental experience. It is a whole-body state, with predictable patterns. When you learn those patterns, you stop taking them personally, and you start working with them.

You don't need to earn calm by being perfect. You don't need to force yourself into composure. You don't need to wait for life to settle down before you start. You can begin by noticing load. You can begin by building buffer. You can begin by meeting activation with support instead of criticism.

Those small acts become evidence, and evidence is what teaches the nervous system something new.

In the next chapter, we'll give you a simple way to understand what is happening inside you in the moments where calm feels least accessible. We'll look at the two parts of the brain that often compete for the steering wheel under stress, and why "just calm down" rarely lands when you need it most.

For now, let this be enough:

You're not behind.

You're not failing.

You're learning a skill most people were never taught.

Chapter 2

THE TWO BRAINS–CAVEMAN AND CEO

If your inner world were a theater, most days would look pretty normal from the outside.

The lights are up. The show is running. You're answering emails, making dinner, parenting, working, talking, doing what needs doing. The audience sees a competent adult holding it together.

But behind the curtain, there's a whole crew keeping that show on the road.

There's the part of you that can think clearly, make decisions, choose words carefully, and take perspective. There's the part that reacts fast, scans for danger, and hits the alarm button before you've worked out what happened. There's the inner critic waiting in the wings with a clipboard, ready to review your performance harshly. There's the calm narrator who shows up later with brilliant insight, usually when it's no longer useful.

And then there are the moments where the stage gets hijacked.

A tone in someone's voice. A vague email. A child's meltdown. A look that lands as judgment. A conversation that suddenly feels unsafe. In one second, your body is tight, your mind is either racing or blank, and you're no longer running the scene the way you intended.

Later, when the moment is over, you can finally see it. You can name it. You can even laugh at it sometimes. "I don't know what came over me." "That wasn't me." "I knew what I wanted to say, but I couldn't access it."

That gap between "in the moment" you and "after" you is the confusing part. It makes people doubt themselves. It makes them feel inconsistent, as if their insight doesn't translate into behavior.

But it isn't inconsistency. It's a shift in who has the microphone.

I'm going to give you a simple cast list that matches your biology. Not as a cute metaphor but as a practical map. When you can name what's happening, stress stops feeling like a character flaw and starts making sense as a nervous system shift.

You start working with the brain you actually have.

Part 1: Meet the Caveman and the CEO

Let's start with the Caveman.

In your brain, the Caveman is the threat-detection system. It includes structures such as the amygdala, which quickly detects potential danger and triggers a protective response, and other fast networks that help your body mobilize before you have time to think it through.

The Caveman is not stupid. It's fast.

It reads cues rather than words: tone, facial expression, uncertainty, exclusion, sudden change, ambiguity. It asks simple questions: Is this safe? Is this risky? Do I need to act? Do I need to brace?

And it is biased toward protection because that bias kept humans alive. If the Caveman overreacts to a false alarm, the cost is discomfort. If it underreacts to a real threat, the cost is far higher. So its safety system is designed to move quickly, even if it sometimes gets it wrong.

When the Caveman thinks something is dangerous, it recruits the body. Stress hormones rise. Heart rate changes. Muscles tighten. Attention narrows. Your system prepares to fight, flee, freeze, or fawn. This happens before you have time to "decide" it should be happening. Physiology first, story later.

Now, meet the CEO.

The CEO lives primarily in the prefrontal cortex, the part of the brain involved in planning, reasoning, inhibition, decision-making, and perspective-taking. It's the part of you that can hold two truths at once, pause and choose, and stay aligned with your values when the moment is emotionally charged.

The CEO is thoughtful, strategic, and can see beyond the next thirty seconds.

It can say, "This is uncomfortable, but it's not dangerous." It can say, "I can respond slowly instead of reacting fast." It can name what's happening and choose a better next step.

But there's a catch. The CEO is slower.

That isn't a flaw. It's the nature of higher-order thinking. Reflection takes time. Language takes time. Nuance takes time. And when your nervous system is in a threat state, your brain prioritizes speed over nuance.

So, under stress, the Caveman tends to grab the microphone, and the CEO loses influence for a while. Not permanently. Just while your brain is in survival mode.

This is why you can be calm five minutes after the moment, but not in it.

It's also why "just calm down" rarely works. When you are activated, you're not speaking to a fully resourced prefrontal cortex. You're speaking into a system that has shifted toward protection. The tools that work vary with activation level because different parts of the brain are available.

And then there are the other characters.

The inner critic often shows up after the fact, when the Caveman has already done its thing. It doesn't help you regulate. It punishes you for not regulating, reviewing your performance as if shame is a training plan.

The calm narrator often appears later, too, when the chemistry has settled, and the CEO is back online. It becomes articulate, insightful, wise. It can suddenly see the bigger picture. The problem is timing. It's hard to access that narrator when your nervous system is still running the emergency program.

Part of learning calm is learning to shift who is holding the mic in real time. You can't force yourself to be rational, but you can help your nervous system to settle enough for the CEO to come back online.

Part 2: Why the CEO Goes Offline – What Stress Does to Thinking, Language, and Choice

If you have ever walked away from a tense moment and thought, *Why couldn't I just say it properly,* you already know what this part is about.

In the moment, you might feel flooded, blank, sharp, small, defensive, urgent, or strangely numb. Your thoughts either race or disappear. Your voice doesn't sound like you. Your body feels tight and hot, or heavy and distant. Then later, when the chemistry settles, your CEO returns, and you can suddenly see what you should have done.

Most people interpret that as a personal failure.

It isn't. It is a predictable shift in brain function under stress.

When the Caveman detects threat, it doesn't only change how you feel. It changes what parts of your brain you can access. The goal of the stress response is to increase your chances of survival, and survival doesn't require nuance. It requires speed, focus, and action.

So the brain reallocates resources. Working memory shrinks, language becomes harder to access, and the brain prioritizes speed and salience over reflection. That's why a stressed mind can feel both urgent and surprisingly uncreative at the same time.

In very simple terms, you can think of it as the theater's power supply being redirected. The emergency lights come on. The spotlight narrows. The stage manager starts yelling orders. The crew stops working on long-term set design and focuses on getting you through the next sixty seconds.

That is what your nervous system does.

The alarm system is fast, and it does not wait for permission.

The amygdala and related threat-detection circuits are designed to pick up cues quickly. They respond to things that resemble danger: not only obvious physical threats but social and relational threats too. A harsh tone, a sudden silence, exclusion, unpredictability, criticism, conflict, embarrassment. These can all register as "not safe" at a nervous system level, even when your rational mind knows you are not in physical danger.

Once the threat system is activated, the body is recruited. Stress hormones such as adrenaline and cortisol increase energy availability, change heart rate and breathing, and sharpen attention toward what matters most right now. This can be helpful if you need to act. It is less helpful if you need to have a nuanced conversation, find the right words, or make a thoughtful decision.

The Caveman does not care about your values in that moment. It cares about protecting you.

Saber-Toothed Tigers and Modern Stress

If you zoom out for a moment, this design makes perfect sense.

The Caveman brain was shaped in a world where most threats were concrete and immediate: a predator on the horizon, a food shortage, an injury, a hostile tribe, exclusion from the group. The stakes were physical, and the cost of missing danger was high. So the nervous system evolved to detect risk quickly and mobilize the body before you have time to debate.

That is why the threat system is built for speed rather than accuracy. It would rather have a false alarm than a missed alarm. A false alarm costs energy. A missed alarm could cost your life.

In other words, your brain was designed for saber-toothed tigers.

The problem is that the threat system doesn't only respond to teeth and claws. It responds to cues that resemble danger in modern life, especially relational cues. A critical tone. A loss of status. The possibility of disapproval. Being singled out in a meeting. Being excluded from a group chat. Receiving an email from your boss with the subject line "Can we talk?" and no context.

Your body reacts first because it's running a very old program: assess threat, mobilize, protect.

Your rational mind might know you are not about to be eaten, but the nervous system isn't deciding between "saber-toothed tiger" and "work email." It's deciding between "safe enough" and "not safe." It treats uncertainty and social threat as real threats because, for most of human history, social safety mattered for survival. Being pushed out of the tribe could be deadly. So the nervous system learned to take relational cues very seriously.

This is why you can feel a jolt in your chest from a message on a screen. The Caveman is not ridiculous. The Caveman is doing what it evolved to do. The issue isn't that the system exists. The issue is that the modern world gives it an endless stream of cues, many of them vague, constant, and difficult to resolve.

The spotlight narrows, and so does your thinking.

One of the first things stress changes is attention.

In threat, attention narrows. Your brain becomes more vigilant. It scans for potential problems and locks onto them. This is why you can become fixated on one detail, one look, one line in an email, one perceived slight. Your brain is trying to identify the threat and respond quickly, and it doesn't have the luxury of taking in the whole picture.

You can also feel this narrowing internally. Your mind starts to loop. You run mental simulations. You rehearse what you should say. You jump to worst-case scenarios. You become less able to hold complexity, to see multiple perspectives, to tolerate uncertainty.

This is not you being irrational. It is your nervous system doing what it is designed to do under stress.

Working memory shrinks, and language can disappear.

The CEO relies heavily on the prefrontal cortex, the brain region that supports planning, inhibition, decision-making, and perspective-taking. It is also a key part of what lets you pause and choose your response rather than react automatically.

Under threat, the prefrontal cortex's influence often decreases. It does not turn off completely, but the brain prioritizes survival networks over reflection networks. The result is that the things the CEO is good at become harder in the moment.

Working memory is a good example. Working memory is the mental "scratch pad" that holds information while you use it. It lets you keep track of what someone just said, what you meant to respond with, what you want the outcome to be, and what matters most to you. Under stress, that scratch pad gets smaller. You lose track mid-sentence. You forget what you were going to say. You can't find words you know you know. You say something and immediately think, "That wasn't what I meant."

Some people experience this as going blank. Some experience it as talking too much. Some experience it as an urge to explain, defend, justify, or fix because the nervous system is trying to regain a sense of safety through control. Either way, it is a sign that the CEO is under-resourced.

State-dependent access is why insight arrives later.

One of the most relieving concepts in nervous system work is this: Access is state-dependent.

You do not have equal access to your best thinking in every state.

When your body is in a threat state, the parts of you that can reflect and choose are less reachable. That is why you can read a book, understand the concept, agree with the idea, and still react the old way in the moment. It is not that the learning did not "stick." The state did not allow you to access it.

Then later, when you are regulated again, the CEO comes back online. You can see options. You can take perspective. You can communicate clearly. You can even feel compassion for the other person. This is why your calm narrator is always so wise on the drive home.

It's not that you suddenly became smarter. It's that the state changed.

This is why "try harder" is the wrong instruction.

If you take one thing from this part, let it be this: You cannot reliably solve a nervous system state with more thinking.

In a threat state, thinking tools are limited because the CEO has less influence. Trying harder often makes it worse because you add frustration and self-judgment on top of the activation. The nervous system hears that as more threat, and the cycle escalates.

That doesn't mean thinking is useless. It means thinking belongs at the right time.

When you are calm enough to access the CEO, thinking is powerful. Reflection is powerful. Reframing is powerful. Communication is powerful.

But when you are activated, the first move is usually to work with the body. You can help the system stand down enough for the CEO to return. Then you can think clearly, choose words well, and act in line with who you want to be.

This is the sequence that changes everything. State first. Then story.

In the next part, we'll make this practical by looking at how to recognize who is holding the microphone in real time, and what it looks like to shift the power back toward the CEO without trying to force it.

Part 3: Who's Holding the Microphone – How to Tell Which Part of Your Brain Is Driving in Real Time

Now that you know why the CEO can go offline under stress, the next step is learning to recognize the shift while it's happening.

This is where the theater metaphor becomes genuinely useful, because it gives you a way to spot what's on stage without needing to diagnose yourself or overthink your feelings. You're not trying to become a perfect observer. You're simply trying to answer one practical question in the moment: Who is holding the microphone right now?

When the CEO is holding the mic, you can usually feel it. You have access to language and choice. You can pause. You can consider the impact of your words. You can tolerate a bit of discomfort without needing to fix it immediately. You might still feel stressed, but you're present.

When the Caveman is holding the mic, everything speeds up and narrows. Your body is leading. You feel urgency. You feel threat. You feel an impulse to do something now, even if "now" is the worst possible time. The story in your head becomes more extreme, and the options feel fewer.

The trick is not to discern which one is on stage. The trick is to recognize the cues early, because early recognition gives you more leverage.

Here are the most common ways you can tell.

The body gives it away first.

The Caveman doesn't arrive as a thought. It arrives as sensation.

You might feel heat in your chest or face. A tightening in your throat. A clench in your jaw. Your shoulders creeping up. A buzzing in your limbs. Restless energy. Or the opposite: a heaviness, a sudden drop, a foggy distance.

Breath often changes, too. It gets higher in the chest or shallower without your noticing. Your heart rate may jump. Your stomach might drop. Your hands might go cold.

None of that means anything is "wrong." It simply means your nervous system is mobilizing. It is preparing you for a saber-toothed tiger, even if the tiger is an email.

Your thinking gets simpler, sharper, or louder.

When the CEO is online, your thoughts tend to have more range. You can hold complexity and nuance. You can think in "both/and" rather than "either/or." You can keep the long game in mind.

When the Caveman takes over, thinking changes.

The mind becomes more binary: right or wrong, safe or unsafe, attack or retreat, fix it now, or it will be terrible. The story can get dramatic quickly because the brain is trying to justify the body's state. It scans for evidence that confirms threat, and it tends to ignore evidence that would soften it.

Sometimes the thoughts get loud and fast. You start rehearsing, planning what you'll say, imagining what they meant, reading between the lines with a threat filter.

Sometimes the thoughts disappear altogether. You go blank. You can't access words. You can't remember what you were going to say. You feel like the floor drops out under your ability to think.

Both are signs that you are in a different brain state, not a different personality.

Your behavior becomes more automatic.

When the CEO is holding the mic, you can choose your response. You might still be direct, emotional, or firm, but there's choice in it.

When the Caveman is holding the mic, behavior becomes reflexive.

For some people, it looks like fight: You interrupt, argue, get sharp, defend, push, become controlling.

For some people, it looks like flight: You want to escape, withdraw, go busy, avoid the conversation, disappear emotionally, or literally leave the room.

For some people, it looks like freeze: You go still, can't speak, can't move, feel stuck and flooded at the same time. You might look calm on the outside while you're in chaos inside.

For some people, it looks like fawn: You become overly agreeable, over-apologize, try to keep the peace at all costs, abandon your own needs to reduce risk.

These are not character flaws. They're protective strategies, the nervous system trying to keep you safe in the way it learned worked best.

The critic and the calm narrator usually show up after.

Two other characters often appear once the moment is already underway.

The inner critic tends to arrive with commentary. It tells you you're ridiculous for feeling what you feel. It says you should handle this better. It tries to shame you into regulation, which is like trying to put out a fire with gasoline. It often makes the state worse, because shame registers as threat.

The calm narrator usually arrives later: on the drive home, in the shower, at 2 a.m. It becomes eloquent and wise once your body is no longer flooded. It can suddenly see what the other person might have meant. It can generate the perfect response. It can explain the whole dynamic.

The calm narrator is not useless. It's actually one of your strengths. It helps you learn from experience and make meaning later. The problem is timing. It's hard to access that narrator when the Caveman is running the show.

That's why the skill is not becoming more insightful. The skill is learning to notice earlier, so you can keep the CEO online longer, or bring it back sooner.

The Simplest Check-In Question

If you want one question that cuts through all of this, use this: "Do I have access to choice right now?"

If the answer is yes, even a little, you're in a workable state. The CEO still has some influence. Small actions will help. You can slow your breath, widen your attention, soften your body, and shift the trajectory.

If the answer is no, you are likely in a higher gear. You don't need to think more. You need stabilization. You need fewer words, less complexity, and more body-based support until you come back into range.

You don't have to label it perfectly. You don't have to get it right every time. You just need to recognize the pattern soon enough to respond with the right kind of support.

Part 4: How to Get the CEO Back on Stage – What Actually Helps When You Can't Just "Calm Down"

Once you can recognize who is holding the microphone, the next question becomes much simpler: What will actually help right now?

This matters because most people reach for the wrong tool at the wrong time. They try to reason with themselves when their body is already in a state of threat. They try to find the perfect words when language is the very thing that has gone offline. They try to calm down by thinking harder, which only adds more fuel.

So let's make this practical.

When the Caveman is running the show, the goal is not to become serene. The goal is to create enough shift in the nervous system that the CEO can regain influence. That usually happens bottom-up. You support the body first, and the mind follows.

Think of it like the theater's lighting system. When the emergency lights are on, you don't argue with the stage manager. You change the conditions. You reduce the alarms. You lower the intensity. You restore the power supply to the parts of the theater that run the main show.

There are three levers that work almost every time because they speak directly to the nervous system's language: breath, attention, and muscle tension.

1. Change the breath to change the signal.

Breathing is one of the few systems in the body that is both automatic and controllable. That makes it a direct bridge between the CEO and the Caveman. You don't use breath because it's magical. You use it because it changes what the nervous system is perceiving.

Short, shallow breathing tells the body, "We are under threat." A slower breath with a slightly longer exhale tells the body, "We can stand down a notch."

You don't need a perfect technique. In real life, simple is better.

Try this: Inhale normally, then exhale a little longer than you inhaled. Do that two or three times. Keep it subtle. No one needs to know you're doing it. You're not trying to become calm instantly. You're sending a different signal long enough for your body to register it.

If you want the simplest instruction possible, it's this: Make the exhale longer.

Exhaling is linked to settling pathways in the nervous system. Lengthening it even slightly can reduce the sense of urgency, which is often what keeps the Caveman gripping the mic.

2. Widen attention to tell the brain, "We're not trapped."

Threat narrows attention. It makes you lock onto the problem: the email, the person's face, the one sentence that hurt, the one thing that could go wrong.

That narrowing is part of the survival program. It helps you respond quickly.

But when you widen attention, you give your nervous system a different message: "There is more here than the threat."

Again, this is not positive thinking. It's physiology.

One simple way to do this is to let your eyes move. Look around the room slowly. Notice shapes, colors, edges. Let your gaze land on neutral objects. Feel your feet on the ground as you do it. This is called orienting, and it's a way of reminding the nervous system that you are here, now, in the present, and that there are options.

If you can't move your eyes much because you're in a conversation, you can still widen your attention internally. Notice your contact with the chair. Notice the temperature of the air on your skin. Notice the weight of your hands. Small, sensory cues bring the brain back into the present, which is where the CEO has the most access.

3. Soften the brace to reduce threat signals.

Most people don't realize they're bracing until they stop.

The jaw tightens. The shoulders rise. The hands grip. The belly holds. The legs lock. You prepare.

The nervous system uses muscle tension as part of its threat calculation. If your body is braced, your brain reads that as evidence that something is wrong. Therefore, one of the fastest ways to send a safety signal is to release one piece of bracing.

Pick one place. Jaw is a good one. So are shoulders and hands.

Unclench the jaw. Drop the shoulders a fraction. Let your hands soften. You don't need to relax your whole body. You're not aiming for floppy. You're aiming for less armor.

Often, that small release creates a cascade because the body stops feeding the alarm system with tension data.

The Mistake to Avoid: Using More Words When Words Are the Problem

When the Caveman is driving, people often try to regain control through language. They explain more. They justify. They defend. They talk faster. They search for the perfect sentence. They argue their way back to safety.

Sometimes this works in the short term, but it often escalates the nervous system. More words can mean more stimulation, more heat, higher stakes.

If you feel yourself getting activated in a conversation, one of the most regulating moves can be to reduce complexity. Fewer words. Shorter sentences. More pauses. You buy time for your body to come down.

This is where a "minimum effective response" becomes your friend.

You don't need to win the conversation while you are flooded. You need to stop the situation from escalating long enough for the CEO to return.

Sometimes the minimum effective response is a simple sentence like, "I need a moment," or "Let me think about that," or "I want to respond well—give me a second." It protects the relationship and creates space without turning into avoidance.

A Practical Way to Remember This in the Moment

If you want a simple structure without turning your life into a worksheet, use this:

1. Name who is on stage. "Caveman is driving."
2. Lower intensity. Longer exhale. Soften one brace. Widen attention.
3. Delay decisions. No big replies. No big conclusions. Buy time.
4. Return to CEO tools. Once you're back in range, then think, speak, decide.

That's it. Not a long sequence. Just a tiny shift in the order you do things.

Because the CEO does not come back through shame. It comes back through safety.

And the more you practice these small moves, the more predictable you become to your own nervous system. Your body learns that it doesn't have to escalate to get support. The Caveman relaxes its grip. The CEO gets more stage time.

In the next part, we'll bring this into real-world situations: the moments where you can't step away, can't take a break, and still need to function like an adult while a saber-toothed tiger is apparently approaching via Outlook.

Part 5: What It Looks Like in Real Life – Keeping the Show Running When the Tiger Arrives Mid-Scene

It's one thing to understand the cast list when you're reading a book in a quiet moment.

It's another thing to remember it when you're in the middle of a meeting, a family dinner, a tense text thread, or a conversation that suddenly turns sharp. Real life doesn't pause, so you can take a mindful moment. The tiger does not wait politely in the wings.

So let's make this concrete.

In the moments that matter most, regulation often looks subtle. It looks like tiny shifts you make inside your body while your face remains fairly normal. It looks like buying enough time for the CEO to come back on stage without creating a bigger mess in the scene.

When You Get an Email from Your Boss, and Your Stomach Drops

This is one of the most common modern saber-toothed tigers. The message is vague. The subject line is ominous. There is no context. Your brain fills in the blanks.

If you've ever felt your heart rate jump before you even open the email, you're not imagining it. Uncertainty is a strong cue for the threat system. Your nervous system would rather prepare for the worst than be caught off guard.

The first move here is not to think. The first move is to stop feeding the alarm with urgency.

Before you reply, give yourself one longer exhale. Feel your feet on the ground. Unclench your jaw. Let your eyes move around the room for a second so your system registers, "I am here, and I am not under attack."

Then do one practical CEO move: Reduce ambiguity.

That might mean reading the email twice before reacting to it. It might mean asking one clarifying question instead of writing a defensive essay. It might mean replying with something simple like, "Sure, happy to chat. What's the context, so I can come prepared?" That is not weakness. That is competence. You're giving your brain more information, so it doesn't have to invent a tiger.

And if you notice your mind racing, treat that as a cue, not a problem. Racing is your system trying to regain control. Bring it back to the body: one longer exhale, one softened shoulder, one deliberate pause before you press send.

When You're in a Meeting, and You Can Feel Yourself Getting Sharp

This is the moment where a lot of capable people lose access to their best selves. Someone challenges you. You feel judged, dismissed, put on the spot. Your body tightens. Your voice changes. You want to interrupt, defend, or prove your point.

The CEO's best move here is not to be perfect. It's to slow the pace.

You can do that without anyone noticing. Let your hands soften on the table. Drop your shoulders a fraction. Lengthen one exhale while the other person is speaking. Allow a beat of silence before you respond.

That beat is not awkward. It is regulatory. It buys the CEO time.

If you need a script, use something that protects you without escalating: "Let me think about that for a moment." "That's an important point. I want to respond properly." "Can you say a bit more about what you're concerned about?" Questions are often a CEO move because they widen attention and reduce threat. They shift you out of defense and into information-gathering.

And if you notice you're already tipping into fight mode, reduce words. Keep sentences shorter. Avoid the urge to explain everything. The goal is not to win the exchange. The goal is to stay online.

When Your Child Is Melting Down, and Your Nervous System Matches Theirs

This is one of the most honest mirrors you will ever have.

A child's distress is loud, intense, and relentless. It triggers urgency in the adult nervous system because your brain reads it as "something is wrong, and it must be fixed now." If you grew up in an environment where emotions were dangerous, or if you have a history of being responsible for other people's feelings, a child's dysregulation can hit an even deeper layer.

The most important thing to know here is that your child's nervous system is not primarily responding to your logic. It's responding to cues of safety.

That doesn't mean you have to become a saint. It means the fastest way to help a child settle is often to stabilize your own body first.

Lower your shoulders. Slow your voice. Lengthen the exhale. Soften your face. Speak fewer words than you feel like speaking. Your body becomes the steady signal in the room.

If you can't do that, you can't do that. Real life is real life. But the goal is not to manage the child with perfect parenting. It is to prevent two nervous systems from escalating each other.

Sometimes the CEO move is creating containment: "I'm here. I'm not going anywhere. We're going to slow this down." Sometimes it's stepping away for a moment if the child is safe, so you don't bring a tiger onto the stage with them.

When You Get Triggered in a Relationship, and the Story Starts Writing Itself

Relational threat is powerful because connection has always been tied to safety. Your nervous system learned early what disconnection, conflict, silence, and criticism mean. Those templates can activate fast, before you've checked whether the present moment actually matches the past.

This is where the microphone question helps.

If you notice the Caveman has it, do not escalate with language. This is where people say things they regret because they're trying to regain a sense of safety through control.

Slow the pace instead. Soften the brace. Take one longer exhale. Ask yourself, "Do I have access to choice right now?" If the answer is no, you don't need to solve the relationship in this state.

A minimum effective response might be, "I'm feeling activated. I don't want to do any damage. Can we pause and come back?" That sentence protects connection and protects the relationship from your threat chemistry.

And when you come back, that's the CEO's time. That's when you can name what you felt, what you needed, and what you want to do differently. But not while the tiger is still on stage.

When You're Alone, Spiraling Internally

Not all tiger moments are loud. Some happen quietly, in your own mind.

You sit down, and suddenly you're running a mental slideshow: what you should have said, what might happen, what they meant, what you need to fix. Your body is tight even though you're alone. Your mind is trying to create certainty because uncertainty feels unsafe.

In these moments, more thinking rarely helps. It tends to keep the system activated.

The CEO move is to change state through the body.

Stand up. Change location. Press your feet into the floor. Let your eyes move around the room. Wash your face or step into fresh air. Lengthen the exhale. Give your nervous system a cue that you are here, now, and not in immediate danger.

Then, and only then, decide what needs your attention. Sometimes the answer is "nothing, I'm spiraling." Sometimes the answer is "one practical step." But you'll see the difference more clearly once the nervous system drops out of emergency gear.

What to Remember

In real life, the skill is not getting rid of the tiger. The skill is recognizing when the tiger has walked on stage and responding in a way that brings the CEO back online sooner.

That response will not always be graceful. It will not always be perfect. But it will become more familiar with practice, because your nervous system learns through repetition.

And the more often you respond to activation with support instead of criticism, the more predictable you become to your own body. Over time, the Caveman starts to relax its grip. It stops assuming every cue is life or death. It stops shouting to be heard.

That's the beginning of real calm. Not performance, not polish, but a nervous system that trusts you to lead the show.

Part 6: The Other Characters

So far, we've talked about the Caveman and the CEO as if they're the only two on stage.

In reality, they're the main systems, but they're not the only characters who show up when stress hits. In many people, activation triggers a familiar supporting cast. These characters aren't random quirks. They're protective strategies, patterns your nervous system learned because, at some point, they helped you stay safe, stay connected, or stay functional.

When you can recognize them, you stop treating them as "who you are," and you start treating them as roles that can be stepped out of.

THE CRITIC

The critic tends to arrive after the Caveman has already reacted.

It shows up as commentary. It analyzes your performance, judges your tone, and tells you what your reaction "means" about you. It points out the flaw, highlights the embarrassing part, predicts the consequences. It tries to make sure you never do that again.

The critic often believes it's helping. It thinks shame will keep you safe. If it punishes you hard enough, maybe you'll finally get it right next time.

But shame is not a regulatory tool.

From a nervous system perspective, self-attack reads as threat. It keeps the body activated. It can even extend the stress response because you're now dealing with two problems at once: the original trigger and the internal judgment about it.

In this situation, critic management is crucial because critic-talk often prevents learning. A useful move here is to name it gently and shift it into a different role.

Instead of "I'm ridiculous," the CEO can say, "My system got activated." Instead of "I ruined everything," the CEO can say, "That was a stress response I can repair." That is not letting yourself off the hook. It's removing the extra threat so you can actually respond.

THE FIXER

The fixer appears when the nervous system equates safety with solving.

It offers solutions, explanations, long messages, quick decisions, and immediate action. It's the part that wants to resolve the discomfort as fast as possible, even if the situation doesn't truly require it, because unresolved tension feels like danger.

The fixer is often highly competent. It has probably served you well in work and relationships. The trouble is that in a threat state, fixing can become a form of control. You start doing things quickly to reduce anxiety, and you can end up creating new problems while trying to solve the old one.

The CEO move with the fixer is to slow it down.

You ask, "Do I actually need to solve this right now?" and "What is the minimum effective response?" Sometimes the minimum effective response is one sentence and a pause. Sometimes it's a clarifying question. Sometimes it's choosing containment over resolution until you're steadier.

Fixing is not wrong. It just needs to happen with the CEO online.

The Pleaser

The pleaser appears when safety equals connection.

This is the part of you that tries to keep things smooth. It over-apologizes, agrees too quickly, edits itself, absorbs responsibility that isn't yours. It tries to prevent disappointment, conflict, or disapproval because your nervous system is reading the cues. It uses appeasement as a protective strategy.

Fawning is the term often used for this in nervous system work, and it's easy to misunderstand. It's not weakness. It's a survival response.

It can be a very old strategy, learned in environments where keeping someone else calm was the safest option available.

The cost of the pleaser is that it often abandons your needs.

The CEO move here is gentle grounding and boundary fixing.

You don't need to become confrontational. You simply need to stay connected to yourself while staying connected to the other person. That might look like pausing before you agree. It might look like saying, "Let me think about that," instead of automatically saying yes. It might look like noticing the urge to smooth things over and choosing a slower response.

Over time, the nervous system can learn a new rule: Connection is possible without self-erasure.

THE DISAPPEARING ACT

Some people protect themselves by withdrawing.

They go quiet, vague, numb. They leave emotionally or physically. Sometimes it looks like being calm, but inside, it's dissociation or shutdown. The system is reducing sensation to cope with overwhelm.

Again, this isn't a moral failing. It's the nervous system applying a strategy that once worked.

The CEO move here is to add small amounts of connection back in, without forcing yourself to perform.

That might be orienting to the room, feeling your feet, naming one thing you can see, giving your system gentle cues that you are safe enough to stay present. If you're in a conversation, it might mean saying, "I'm here, I just need a moment," instead of disappearing completely.

The Calm Narrator

The calm narrator is the part of you that becomes wise after the moment has passed.

It shows up with perfect clarity, usually once your nervous system has come down. It can see patterns, explain what you were feeling, understand what the other person might have meant, offer perspective. It can even be funny, which is often a sign of returning to safety.

The calm narrator is not the enemy. It's a resource.

The mistake is expecting the calm narrator to show up while the Caveman has the mic. That's not how nervous systems work. Insight is state-dependent. The calm narrator tends to arrive when the CEO has access again.

So instead of forcing insight in the moment, the skill is learning to stabilize enough to buy access. Then you can use the narrator well, not as a weapon against yourself but as a guide for learning.

Why This Matters

When you recognize these characters, you stop treating your stress responses as your identity.

You start seeing them as roles that appear under certain conditions.

That makes change possible because you can practice a new response while still respecting the fact that the old response once had a reason.

You don't need to fire the cast. You need to become the director.

And directing starts with knowing who has walked onto the stage.

CLOSING: BECOMING THE DIRECTOR

If you take nothing else from this chapter, take this.

When you react under stress, it isn't proof that you're immature or broken. It's proof that your nervous system is working exactly as it was designed to work. A fast threat system detects cues, mobilizes the body, and temporarily reduces access to the parts of the brain that do reflection and language. That shift can feel as though you've been hijacked, but it's not random. It's biology.

This is why good intentions are not enough.

Your CEO can have brilliant plans and still lose the microphone when the Caveman senses danger. That isn't failure. It's a predictable state shift. And when you understand the cast list, you stop arguing with yourself as if you should be one consistent version of you in every moment.

You become curious instead, and the questions get simpler: Who is on stage right now? What does my body think is happening? What would help my system stand down a notch so I can access choice again?

That is the work. Not control. Not perfection. Not performing calm. Supporting the nervous system so you can lead yourself back into range.

The supporting characters matter too. The critic, the fixer, the pleaser, the disappearing act. They aren't personality defects. They're roles you learned, often early, and often for good reason. The goal isn't to shame them off the stage. The goal is to recognize them, thank them for trying to help, and choose a different move when you can.

Over time, those small moves become evidence: evidence that you can pause, that you can repair, that you can be activated and still stay connected to yourself.

That's how the nervous system updates. Not through lectures but through repeated experience.

In the next chapter, we're going to take this one layer deeper. We'll look at what emotions are actually doing, why they feel so convincing, and how to work with them without being ruled by them. Once you understand the job emotions are trying to do, you stop treating them as enemies and start using them as information.

Chapter 3

THE EMOTIONAL OPERATING SYSTEM

Why Feelings Show Up in the Body First

It usually starts as something small.

A tightness in the throat while you're still smiling. A heaviness in the chest you can't explain yet. A flicker of irritation that lands before you've even decided what you think. A sudden urge to check your phone again, as if information itself might make you feel safer.

Then your mind arrives and starts building a story to match the sensation.

> "That was rude."
> "I'm failing."
> "They're disappointed in me."
> "I'm too much."
> "I'm not enough."
> "Something bad is coming."

Most people assume the story caused the feeling. But often it is the other way around. The body shifts first. Then the mind explains it.

That reversal matters because it changes how you work with emotions.

If you believe emotions are purely mental, you will keep trying to manage them with thinking. You will try to talk yourself out of a feeling that began as physiology. You will try to reason with a nervous system state. You will tell yourself you're being silly, dramatic, irrational, or "too sensitive," and then feel worse because the emotion does not immediately obey.

So, let's start with a different premise: Emotions are not personality defects. They are biological signals.

They are part of a system designed to keep you alive, connected, and oriented. They are messages from the body about needs, values, safety, and social belonging. They do not always feel convenient, but they are rarely random. When you learn to read them properly, they become less chaotic and more predictable.

This isn't about becoming endlessly calm or emotionally flat. It's about making emotions make sense and learning the difference between a feeling that is information and a feeling that is being amplified by a stressed state. If you become fluent in your inner operating system, you stop treating every surge as a personal failure.

Because here is the truth most people have never been taught: Your body feels first. Your mind interprets second. And your behavior follows what feels true in that state.

Once you understand that sequence, you stop trying to fix emotions at the wrong level. You start working with the system that produces them.

Part 1: What Emotions Actually Are – Signals, Not Flaws

If someone was never taught a map, they don't become bad at navigating. They simply keep getting lost.

A lot of adults have been handed the emotional equivalent of "Good luck." They were told to calm down, toughen up, stop overreacting, be more resilient, be more grateful, be less sensitive, be more confident. Some were praised for being "easy" and "low maintenance," which often meant they learned to hide what they felt. Others were labeled dramatic, needy, angry, or too much, and learned to judge themselves for being human.

So, it makes sense that emotions can feel like a problem to manage.

But emotions are not a moral verdict or evidence that you are failing at life. They are part of a communication system. Your brain and body are continuously answering questions like:

Am I safe?
Am I connected?
Am I respected?
Am I overloaded?
Do I need to act, rest, speak, move, protect, or repair?

Your emotional state is one of the main ways those answers arrive.

From a neuroscience perspective, emotions are not located in one neat "emotion center." They emerge from networks that integrate body sensations, memory, prediction, and context. Your brain takes in information from inside you (breath, heart rate, muscle tension, gut sensations) and outside you (tone of voice, facial expressions, uncertainty, exclusion), and then generates an emotional experience that helps you respond.

This is why emotions feel physical.

You do not just think anxiety. You feel it as tightness, urgency, scanning, and restless energy.

You do not just think sadness. You feel it as heaviness, slowed movement, a lump in the throat.

You do not just think anger. You feel heat, tension, pressure, a readiness to push back.

Those sensations are not add-ons. They are the core of the signal.

One of the key players here is interoception, your brain's ability to sense what is happening inside your body. Regions such as the insula help translate body signals into conscious experience. When interoceptive signals are strong, emotions feel louder. When you are tired, hungry, overstimulated, or stressed, those signals become more intense. That is not weakness. That is the system turning up the volume because it thinks something matters.

This is also why telling yourself to "just calm down" can be so unhelpful.

The CEO brain can understand the instruction. The body often can't.

If your heart is racing and your breathing is shallow, the body is receiving a threat signal. If your muscles are braced and your attention is locked, the body is preparing for action. In that moment, asking yourself to simply calm down is like asking your smoke alarm to stop beeping while the room is full of smoke.

The alarm is not being dramatic. It is responding to the input it has.

So the skill is not to argue with the alarm but to understand what it's signaling and respond at the right level.

Here is where people get tripped up: They treat emotions as if they are purely about the situation. But emotions are also about state.

The same email can feel neutral on a good day and catastrophic on a depleted one. The same comment can roll off your back when you are resourced and hit like a punch when your baseline is already elevated. The same parenting moment can feel manageable when you have slept and unbearable when you have not.

Your nervous system is sensitive to context, which is exactly what it is designed to be. This doesn't mean you are inconsistent. This is the beginning of emotional literacy. Instead of asking only, "What happened?" or "Why am I like this?" you start also asking, "What state am I in?" or "What is my system responding to?"

Rather than judging the emotion, get curious about the signal.

You can see this in everyday moments.

Say someone asks you a simple question and you feel a flash of defensiveness. Before your mind finds the reason, your body has already decided, "This is a threat to my competence."

Your child sighs and rolls their eyes, and you feel a surge of anger that surprises you. Before your mind can narrate it, your body has already interpreted it as disrespect or loss of control.

Your partner goes quiet, and you feel panic. Before your mind can gather facts, your body is reacting to the possibility of disconnection.

Often, the story that follows will sound convincing because it is being powered by a real physiological shift. The body changes the lens. The lens changes the meaning. The meaning changes the emotion. Then the emotion drives behavior.

This is why emotional intelligence without nervous system understanding can feel like trying to steer a car by arguing with the steering wheel.

You can learn all the labels in the world and become very good at explaining why you feel what you feel, but if you can't recognize the state shift underneath, you will still get pulled into reactions that feel bigger than your intentions.

So we are going to build this chapter around a gentler and more useful truth: Emotions are signals. They are telling you something about safety, connection, load, needs, and values. When you learn the language, you stop being frightened of your own inner life.

One more important clarification: Signals are not always instructions.

Just because you feel urgency does not mean you must act urgently. If you feel shame, it doesn't mean you've done something shameful. Feeling fear does not mean you are in danger.

A signal is information, and the skill is learning how to read it, and then choosing what to do with it when your CEO is actually online.

That is the work of calm. Not suppressing feelings or performing composure. Learning how to stay present with your internal data so you can respond from choice rather than reflex. That's an important distinction. You can't control the emotions you feel. But what you do after that first sixty seconds is absolutely a choice! And you can make a different choice.

The next step is learning to catch emotions earlier, before the story hardens around them. Without analyzing yourself to death, but by noticing the first physical cues. Once you can do that, emotions stop feeling like sudden ambushes and start feeling like signals you can meet.

Part 2: Body First, Story Second – Where Emotions Actually Begin

Most people think they notice an emotion when they notice a thought.

> "I'm annoyed."
> "I'm anxious."
> "I'm upset."
> "I feel rejected."

But if you slow it down, what usually happens is this: Your body shifts first. Then your mind arrives and starts explaining the shift.

That explanation might be accurate, or it might be your nervous system's best guess, made quickly, under pressure, with incomplete information. Either way, the story tends to feel convincing because it is riding on real chemistry. When the body changes, the mind interprets through a different lens. The lens becomes the narrative, which becomes your mood, and then your behavior follows.

So if you want more choice in your emotional life, the most useful place to intervene is earlier than most people think. Not at the level of the story, after you've already spiraled, but at the level of sensation, when the emotion is still forming.

This is the part that sounds simple but changes everything: Emotions begin as physical cues.

Sometimes those cues are obvious. Your chest tightens. Your stomach drops. Heat rises in your face. Your heart rate jumps. Your breath gets shallow. Your shoulders creep up. Your jaw clamps. You feel a fizzing energy in your limbs. Or you feel the opposite: a kind of heaviness, fog, or collapse.

Sometimes the cues are subtle. A slight tension behind the eyes. A shift in posture. A sense of urgency that doesn't have a clear reason. A sudden need to check, fix, do, or prove. A tightening in your throat before you speak.

These are not random sensations. They are your nervous system doing what it always does: scanning for what matters and predicting what happens next, then preparing you accordingly.

You already know this principle from earlier: Your system is always making fast safety assessments beneath conscious awareness. That scanning happens through cues, not logic. Tone, pace, expression, proximity, uncertainty, inclusion, exclusion. It happens through your own internal signals too: how much sleep you've had, whether you're hungry, how much stimulation you've absorbed today, whether you've had any space to recover.

Those cues combine into a state which, in turn, shapes emotion.

This is why the same situation can land differently depending on what your body is carrying.

A comment that feels neutral when you're resourced can feel cutting when you're depleted. A small inconvenience can feel like the last straw when your nervous system is already running hot, and a bit of uncertainty can feel unbearable when you have no buffer left.

Your system is context-sensitive, as it should be.

The Body Signal That Becomes the Story

Here's a common pattern.

Something happens: a look, a tone, a delay, a question that feels slightly pointed. Before you can decide what it means, your body registers it. Your heart rate shifts. Your breath changes. Your muscles brace. Your attention narrows.

Then your mind tries to make sense of the sensation. It reaches for meaning.

> "He's annoyed with me."
> "She thinks I'm incompetent."
> "I've done something wrong."
> "They're going to leave."
> "This is going to get messy."

The story might not be true, but it will feel true because your body is acting as if it is.

This is why trying to "think positively" often fails. You're trying to place a new story on top of a state that is already telling a different story through sensation.

So the first skill here is not reframing. It's noticing. Noticing the earliest physical shift, before your mind turns it into a full narrative.

That's not always easy, because most of us were trained to override the body. We were trained to stay polite, productive, composed, functional. Over time, body signals become background noise until they're so loud we can't ignore them.

This is why building calm starts with learning your own early cues. Not in a performative way but in a practical way.

What Early Cues Look Like in Real Life

Let's make this more tangible.

Jason reads the email subject line, "Quick chat?" and his stomach drops. His thoughts start racing immediately, but the thought-racing is not the start of the emotion. The start is the stomach drop. The thought-racing is the mind trying to stabilize by predicting. It's the CEO trying to regain control after the nervous system has already shifted into threat.

Hannah hears her child's voice escalate in the supermarket and feels heat rise in her chest before she says a single word. That heat is the signal. The irritation that follows is partly about the situation, but it is also about capacity. If she's been juggling decisions and stimulation all day, her nervous system is already close to its threshold. The same moment on a rested day might land differently.

Lena sees her partner walk away and feels a tightening behind her ribs. The mind rushes in with meaning, but the tightening is the start. It's the body's cue that connection feels uncertain. If she learns to notice that tightening early, she has a better chance of choosing what she does next, instead of being dragged into the old story automatically.

These examples matter because they train your attention in the right direction. Early cues usually aren't poetic. They're often mundane, and that's why we miss them. It might be the moment your breath lifts into your chest, or the instant your jaw tightens without your noticing. It might be a subtle bracing through your shoulders, a rush of urgency in your body, or that sinking drop in your stomach that arrives before your mind has a chance to argue.

Sometimes it's not even a clear sensation. It's just a small internal "uh-oh." A shift in the room. A sense of narrowing, as though your attention has snapped onto something. That "uh-oh" is often the doorway because it shows up right at the moment the nervous system starts writing the story.

Why This Matters for Calm

If you catch an emotion early, it's easier to work with because you're meeting it when it's still forming. The nervous system hasn't fully committed yet. You have more access to choice. The story hasn't become a courtroom argument in your head. The chemistry hasn't fully peaked.

When you catch it late, the emotion is already large. The mind is already convinced. The body is already mobilized. And then you're trying to regulate from the steep part of the hill.

You don't need to become hyper-vigilant or analyze every sensation. Rather, get familiar with your personal early-warning system, and emotions will stop surprising you as often.

If you can notice, you can respond, and that response doesn't need to be complicated.

It might be as simple as a longer exhale, a softening of your jaw, a widening of your gaze, or a pause before you speak. Sometimes it's taking a sip of water and letting your body register a small cue of steadiness, or perhaps it's naming the state quietly to yourself: "My system is shifting." Not a dramatic statement, but a cue of orientation. A reminder that you're dealing with physiology, not personal failure.

And sometimes the most powerful response is delaying action.

Because you know that decisions made from a threatened state tend to end in regret. By pausing, you're letting the chemistry come down enough that the CEO can actually participate.

This is the foundation of emotional regulation. Not suppressing what you feel, or performing composure while your body is bracing underneath. It's learning to notice earlier and respond with a little more care, so the nervous system doesn't have to escalate to be heard.

Because emotions aren't the enemy, remember? They're signals. When you treat them as information instead of a problem to eliminate, you get your choice back sooner.

When you learn the language of your body, you stop being blindsided by your own experience. You start meeting it sooner and steering earlier. And the story no longer has to be written by the most activated part of your brain.

Part 3: Neuroception – When Your Nervous System Decides Before You Do

Here's the strange thing about emotions. They can arrive with certainty before you have any evidence.

You can walk into a room and feel on edge without being able to explain why. You can read a message and feel a spike of dread even though the words are polite. You can sit down to relax and feel restless, as if your body didn't get the memo that the day is over.

That experience can make people feel a bit crazy. The mind goes looking for a reason because the mind hates unassigned feelings. If there's a sensation, there must be a story. If there's a surge, there must be a cause.

But often the cause isn't a conscious thought. It's a nervous system assessment.

Your body is constantly scanning for safety and danger, and it does it faster than your conscious mind can keep up. It uses cues that live below language: tone, pace, facial expression, proximity, uncertainty, hierarchy, whether someone feels present or withdrawn, whether you feel included or exposed.

This happens automatically. You're not paranoid; it's how humans stay alive and stay connected. For most of human history, being able to read people quickly was not a social skill. It was a survival skill.

Researchers call this process **neuroception**. It's the nervous system's way of evaluating risk and safety without needing you to think about it. It's your biology doing pattern recognition in the background.

When neuroception detects safety, your system has more access to openness. Social connection feels easier. Breath deepens. Your voice steadies. Your attention widens. You can think more flexibly.

But when neuroception detects danger, your system shifts to protect you. Your attention narrows, and your muscle tone changes. Your breath changes, and your emotional world gets louder. The Caveman is scanning the horizon for tigers, and the CEO has to work harder to stay online.

The tricky part is that neuroception isn't only scanning for obvious threats. It's scanning for cues that predict what tends to happen next.

That means the nervous system can respond to present-day cues as if they are older cues. It can read a tone as criticism because it resembles a tone that once preceded punishment, or read silence as abandonment because silence once meant disconnection. A raised eyebrow becomes judgment because judgment used to cost you safety or belonging.

A Real-Life Example: The Misread Tone

Imagine you're having a perfectly good day. You feel grounded and steady. You ask your partner a simple question and they respond with a tone that's ever so slightly clipped. Not rude. Not hostile. Just . . . off.

Before you have time to think, your stomach drops. Your face warms. Your mind leaps ahead to analyze, fix, or defend. "What did I do? Are they annoyed? Did I miss something?" From the outside, the reaction looks bigger than the moment.

What's happening isn't mysterious. Your nervous system just detected a cue it recognizes: a pattern linked to old experiences of tension, criticism, conflict, or withdrawal. The tone isn't the threat. The association is.

This is why emotions can feel "bigger than the moment," even when you can't point to a dramatic trigger. The nervous system isn't reacting to the sentence. It's reacting to the pattern.

Why You Can't Talk Your Body Out of It

Once you understand neuroception, you stop expecting your body to respond to logic at the speed you'd like.

If your system detects threat, your physiology changes first. Your mind can absolutely help you interpret what's happening, but it's not always the first responder. And if you try to force a cognitive solution before your body has shifted, it can feel like you're arguing with a smoke alarm that is still going off. You can say, "It's fine" as many times as you like. If the system believes it's not fine, it will keep behaving as if something matters.

This is why emotional regulation is often a two-step dance: First, you work with the state. You offer the body enough steadiness that the intensity comes down and the Caveman stands down. Then you work with the meaning. Perspective becomes available again. The CEO can actually participate.

That doesn't mean you have to perform elaborate techniques. Often, the body responds to surprisingly small cues once you know what you're aiming for.

A slower exhale. A softer jaw. A grounded posture. A wider gaze. A small reduction in urgency. A decision not to reply immediately. A moment of orienting, letting your eyes move around the room and land on something neutral.

Those cues tell neuroception, "We are here. We are not trapped. There is no tiger. We can stand down a notch."

THE THREE PLACES NEUROCEPTION LISTENS

Neuroception doesn't only scan the outside world. It listens in three directions at once: the environment, relationships, and your internal state.

The environment is the easiest to understand: crowded spaces, noise, harsh lighting, constant interruptions, no privacy, no time to reset. Those conditions don't always look like danger, but they raise your baseline. Your system stays slightly braced because it's managing input all the time.

Relationships are even more powerful. The nervous system pays attention to the cues that signal connection is stable or unstable. Tone, pace, being misunderstood, and feeling dismissed all matter. So do warmth, eye contact, laughter, repair, and being met with steadiness when you're not at your best. These aren't "soft" factors. They are physiological safety cues.

Then there's internal state. This is the one most people forget, and it explains so much.

When you're hungry, sleep-deprived, overstimulated, hormonal, in pain, or running on caffeine and willpower, your nervous system is already closer to its threshold. In that state, your system is more likely to interpret cues as threatening because your body is already under strain. Neuroception is always doing cost-benefit calculations. When resources are low, the system becomes more conservative.

This is why you can handle the same situation beautifully one day and fall apart the next. The situation didn't change, but your internal conditions did.

And once you see that, you stop making the emotional swing mean something about your character, and you start treating it like physiology.

What It Looks Like When Neuroception Runs the Show

A lot of the time, neuroception doesn't show up as a dramatic emotion. It shows up as a subtle shift in behavior. You might notice yourself explaining more than necessary, as if clarity could prevent conflict. You might start scanning for tiny signs that someone is upset, reading tone and pauses as if they contain hidden meaning. You might feel a pressure to fix things quickly, to smooth the moment, to make the tension go away before it turns into something worse.

For some people, it looks sharper. You get snappier than usual, more impatient, less generous in your interpretation of others. For others, it looks quieter. You go still, you go blank, you disappear internally while continuing to function on the outside. You might feel the familiar pull toward people-pleasing, controlling the situation, or withdrawing altogether because they are the moves your nervous system has learned to associate with safety.

Seen through that lens, these behaviors aren't random habits. They're protective strategies. They're your system trying to guide you back toward safety and connection, using the patterns it already knows.

This is also why it's so hard to "just be present" when you're activated. Presence requires safety. If your nervous system has detected danger, your attention will move toward threat monitoring because that is what it's designed to do.

So when someone says, "Just relax," the nervous system hears, "Ignore your threat detection," which is not a request it accepts easily. The Caveman takes his job very seriously!

A more useful approach is: "What cue of safety can I offer right now?"

Sometimes that cue is internal: a softer breath, a less braced posture, a reminder that you can take time.

Or that cue might be relational: a calmer tone, a slower pace, a simple repair, a sentence that protects connection without over-explaining.

If the cue is environmental, it looks like fewer inputs, a quieter space, a moment outside, turning the brightness down, closing one tab, literally and metaphorically.

It's about becoming fluent in what your system responds to so you can guide it rather than fight it.

THE POINT OF NAMING NEUROCEPTION

You don't need the word "neuroception" to live a calmer life. But naming it can be surprisingly relieving because it gives you a clean explanation for something many people experience and quietly judge themselves for.

It explains why you can feel an emotion arrive before you've had a single conscious thought. It explains why your body can register "not safe" even when your rational mind knows there's no real danger. It helps make sense of why certain people, places, and tones can shift your state so quickly, and why warmth, steadiness, and repair in relationships can be so powerfully regulating.

It also shines a light on why self-judgment is such an unhelpful companion here. Shame is interpreted by the nervous system as threat, and threat turns the volume up on everything. When you pile criticism on top of activation, you don't get calmer. You get more braced.

Most importantly, this gives you a different kind of compassion. Not the kind that excuses harmful behavior, or the kind that collapses into helplessness. The kind that says, "Ah. This is a nervous system event. My body is doing what it learned to do." And from that place, your next move becomes steadier, simpler, and far more effective.

That compassion changes your next move. You stop trying to win an argument with your own biology, and you start offering support.

And when you do that consistently, something subtle shifts over time. Neuroception updates. The system learns new cues, the threshold changes, and the feeling of being constantly on alert begins to soften because your nervous system becomes less convinced that every signal is a threat.

You start living with more range. More access to choice and the ability to feel what you feel without being dragged around by it.

That's when emotional regulation stops being a performance and becomes a relationship with your own system.

Part 4: The Two Questions That Change Everything – How to Work with Emotions Without Being Run by Them

Once you understand that emotions begin in the body and that neuroception is constantly scanning in the background, looking for tigers, the goal shifts. You stop treating emotions like problems to eliminate and start treating them like information to work with.

That doesn't mean you have to welcome every feeling with open arms. Some emotions are intense, messy, inconvenient. Some arrive at the worst possible time and feel like they will swallow you if you let them in.

The point is not to become someone who never feels those things but to know what to do when you do feel them.

People get stuck because they ask the wrong question. They ask, "How do I stop feeling this?" or "How do I calm down right now?" Those questions make sense, but they often create a fight with your own experience. And fighting an emotion usually adds threat, which makes the system louder.

A more useful approach is simpler.

When an emotion shows up, there are two questions that change the whole interaction.

The first is: What is this feeling trying to protect?

Underneath most big emotions is some form of protection. Fear protects you from danger. Anger protects your boundaries. Shame protects belonging. Sadness protects what matters. Even numbness protects you from overload. Emotions are rarely random. They show up because your system believes something important is at stake.

If you can get curious about what the emotion is protecting, you stop treating it as an enemy. You begin to understand what it is doing for you, even if you don't love the way it's doing it.

The second question is: What does my nervous system need right now?

This is the practical question. It shifts you out of analysis and into support. It recognizes that your ability to respond wisely depends on state. If your body is braced, your thinking will be narrow. If your breath is shallow, your mind will feel urgent. If your system feels unsafe, your inner critic will get loud.

Remember, the goal is helping the body stand down a notch, so you can access choice again.

These two questions work together. The first helps you understand meaning without shame. The second helps you respond at the level the nervous system can receive.

What This Looks Like in Real Time

Imagine you're about to send a message and you feel a surge of urgency. Your fingers want to type quickly. Your mind is already rehearsing. Your body feels tight.

If you ask, "What is this feeling trying to protect?" you might realize it's protecting you from uncertainty. It's trying to regain control, and it wants reassurance now.

If you ask, "What does my nervous system need right now?" the answer might be: Slow down. Exhale. Delay action. Let the urgency drop before you press send.

That one shift can change the whole outcome.

Or imagine you're in a conversation and you feel yourself getting defensive. Your chest tightens. Your tone sharpens. You want to explain yourself immediately because your system is trying to prevent misunderstanding from becoming rejection.

"What is this feeling trying to protect?" might reveal a need for respect, fairness, or being seen accurately.

"What does my nervous system need right now?" might be fewer words, a slower pace, a grounded posture, and a pause before responding. You can still speak, but you speak from a steadier state.

Or imagine you feel shame after a mistake. The critic arrives fast. Your mind starts running the self-attack script. You want to hide or overcompensate.

"What is shame trying to protect?" is often about belonging. It's the nervous system's ancient attempt to keep you included by preventing you from doing something that might cost you connection.

"What does my nervous system need right now?" might be gentleness, containment, and a reminder that mistakes are not emergencies. Shame wants isolation. Regulation brings you back toward connection, with yourself first.

How to Tell the Difference Between a Signal and a Spiral

These questions also help you separate two different things that often get tangled: the emotion itself and the story your mind builds around it.

The signal is usually clean. Fear, anger, sadness, disappointment. You can feel it in the body. It has a shape.

The spiral is what happens when the mind starts feeding the signal with additional threat. It piles on prediction, judgment, rehearsal, catastrophic meaning. It turns one moment into a ten-page argument in your head. The spiral doesn't usually bring relief. It increases activation.

So when you're trying to work with emotion, it helps to ask one more distinguishing question: "Am I with the feeling, or am I feeding the story?"

Being with the feeling might look like noticing your breath, letting your shoulders drop, and feeling the sensation without immediately solving it.

Feeding the story often looks like replaying, proving, defending, planning, imagining what they meant, imagining what they'll do, imagining what it says about you.

You don't need to stop these thoughts entirely, but you want to know which direction you're moving: toward regulation or toward escalation.

The skill is not "fixing it." It's staying connected.

This is where people get disappointed, because they want emotional regulation to mean feel something, use a tool, feel better.

Sometimes it works like that, and an exhale and a pause are enough; sometimes naming the feeling reduces its power, or changing your posture or your pace shifts your state quickly.

But often the deeper win is not that the emotion disappears; it's that you stay connected to yourself while it's there.

You can feel anger without becoming cruel, and feel fear without making a panicked decision, and feel sadness without collapsing into hopelessness; you can feel shame without letting it define you, and feel uncertainty without it demanding immediate resolution.

That is regulation: It's not the absence of emotion, but the presence of choice.

And the more often you practice responding to emotions this way, the more your nervous system starts to trust you. It learns that feelings don't have to become emergencies in order to be met. It learns that you don't have to attack yourself to stay safe and that you can feel something intense and still come back to yourself.

Over time, that trust becomes baseline change. The same emotions still arrive, because you're human, but you now have a way to meet them that works with your biology, not against it.

PART 5: WHEN EMOTIONS GET "STUCK" – WHY SOME FEELINGS PASS AND OTHERS LOOP

If emotions are signals, why do some of them move through quickly, while others seem to camp out in your body for days?

Why do you sometimes feel a wave of sadness, cry, and then feel lighter, while at other times, sadness turns into a dull ache that follows you around?

Why can you feel anger, set a boundary, and move on, but other anger becomes a simmering loop that keeps resurfacing in your mind at 2 a.m.?

This is one of the most confusing parts of emotional life, and it's where people start to doubt themselves. They assume that if an emotion isn't passing, they must be doing something wrong. They tell themselves they should be "over it." They try to distract harder, think harder, and fix harder. And the harder they push, the more stuck it feels.

But emotions don't get stuck because you're weak. They get stuck when the signal hasn't been received or when the nervous system doesn't yet feel safe enough to complete what it started.

In simple terms, there are a few common reasons why a feeling loops.

It could be that the emotion is trying to solve a real problem that still exists. You can't regulate your way out of a situation that is objectively unsafe, unjust, or unsustainable. If a boundary needs to be set, if a conversation needs to happen, if a decision needs to be made, the emotion may keep returning because it's still relevant information.

Sometimes the emotion is mixed with threat chemistry. The signal is real, but it's amplified by state. When your baseline is already elevated, everything feels louder. That doesn't mean the emotion is false. It means it's happening in a system that is already braced. In that state, the mind is more likely to ruminate, catastrophize, and look for certainty. The emotion loops because the body doesn't have enough safety to let it move on.

It might be that the emotion is blocked. Not intentionally, but habitually. Many people have learned to swallow feelings quickly because it was safer, more acceptable, or more productive. You cut off the anger before it reaches its message. You override sadness before it can land. You explain away disappointment. You numb fear with busyness. The problem is blocked signals don't disappear. They tend to return as tension, irritability, fatigue, or a vague sense of being "not okay" without knowing why.

And sometimes the emotion is old. The present moment has touched something that was never fully processed when it first happened, and your system is reacting not only to now, but to what now resembles. The feeling is bigger because there is more than one layer to it. There is the current situation, and there is the template it activates.

This is where emotional regulation becomes less about quick relief and more about relationship. The question shifts from "How do I get rid of this?" to "What is this feeling asking for?"

The Difference Between Processing and Ruminating

One of the biggest traps people fall into is confusing rumination with processing.

Rumination feels like you're working on the problem. Your mind replays conversations. It builds arguments. It searches for the perfect explanation. It predicts what might happen next. It tries to gain control through mental rehearsal.

But rumination rarely brings relief. It usually keeps the body activated. It keeps neuroception scanning. It keeps you braced.

Processing is different.

Processing is when you can stay present with the signal long enough to understand what it's asking for, without escalating the threat response. It has a beginning, a middle, and an end. You feel it in the body. You name it. You let it move. You take a small action that aligns with the message. And then, often, the intensity reduces.

A simple way to tell the difference is to ask, "Is this bringing me closer to clarity or keeping me stuck in urgency?"

Rumination often feels urgent and circular. Processing often feels slower and more grounded, even when it's painful.

How Emotions Complete

This part is important because most people were never taught it.

Emotions are designed to move. They rise, peak, and fall. They mobilize the body for action or connection. They carry information. And when the signal has been received, and the nervous system feels safe enough, they complete.

Completion doesn't mean the situation is fixed. It means the emotion has delivered its message, and your system has had enough support to release the intensity.

Sometimes completion happens through expression: a good cry that leaves you softer, a conversation where you finally say what needed to be said, a laugh that releases tension.

Or it might happen through action: setting a boundary, taking a step, making a decision, repairing a relationship, resting when you've been ignoring your limits.

Alternatively, completion might happen through presence: You let yourself feel the sensation without fighting it, stay connected to your breath and your body, stop telling yourself it's wrong to feel it, allow it to be there long enough that it doesn't have to keep knocking.

And sometimes completion happens through the body first, not through insight: a walk that shifts the chemistry, movement that discharges mobilized energy and shakes out the tension, a long exhale that tells the system it can stand down.

This is why "just distract yourself" often fails in the long term. Distraction can help in the short term, especially when you need to function. But if the signal never gets received, it tends to return. The body wants completion, not avoidance.

When the Message Is Hard to Hear

Some signals are uncomfortable because they require change.

Anger might be telling you something isn't okay. That you've over-accommodated. That a boundary is needed. That you're carrying resentment because you've been saying yes when you mean no.

Sadness might be telling you something matters. That there has been loss, or disappointment, or longing. That you need to grieve what didn't happen. That you need tenderness, not toughness.

Fear might be telling you you're overstretched. That you need support. That you need to slow down and reduce load, or you need to create safety before you can take the next step.

Shame might be telling you that you care about belonging. But it often overreaches. Shame is a very blunt instrument, and it frequently tries to protect belonging by attacking you. This is one of the places where the CEO has to step in and offer a different kind of correction, one that keeps you connected rather than collapsing.

The point isn't to obey every feeling. It is to listen long enough to understand what it's doing. When you can hear the signal clearly, you're less likely to get stuck in the loop.

And if a feeling keeps returning, instead of treating it as proof you're failing, you can treat it as information that something hasn't yet been met.

That shift alone reduces the fight. And when the fight reduces, emotions often start to move again.

Part 6: A Simple Way to Work with Any Emotion – The Practice of Name, Notice, Need

By now, the pattern should be clear. Emotions are not random. They are signals shaped by state, context, and history. When you work with them at the right level, they tend to move. When you fight them, shame them, or try to outthink them, they often get louder.

The problem is that in real life, you don't want a long process. You want something you can actually remember when you're activated. Something that works in the kitchen, in the car, in a meeting, in the middle of parenting chaos, or at 2 a.m. when your mind is trying to solve the universe.

So here is a simple practice that fits inside real life. It's not a magic trick. It's a way of relating to emotion that keeps you connected to yourself and gives your nervous system a clear response.

NAME. NOTICE. NEED.

Not as a perfect sequence you have to perform, but as a loose rhythm you can return to.

NAME

Naming is not about labeling an emotion with perfect accuracy. You're not taking a test. You're simply giving your CEO enough language to orient. When you name what's happening, you reduce the sense of being ambushed.

It can be as simple as:

> "I'm feeling anxious."
> "I'm feeling irritated."
> "I feel hurt."
> "I feel overwhelmed."
> "This is shame."
> "This is grief."
> "This is fear."

Sometimes naming is even simpler:

> "My system is activated."
> "This is a stress response."

That kind of naming matters because it changes your relationship to the feeling. Instead of being the feeling, you are noticing the feeling. You are back in the role of director, not just actor.

Notice

Notice is where you bring attention to the body. Not to analyze it but to locate the signal. Where is it? What is it doing? What is the intensity?

You might notice tightness in the throat, pressure in the chest, heat in the face, tension in the jaw, buzzing in the limbs, a sinking feeling in the stomach. You might notice your breath is high and fast. You might notice your posture is braced. You might notice your attention has narrowed.

This is not about "fixing" it instantly. It's about contacting reality. The body is already in the conversation. Notice is you joining it, rather than being dragged by it.

There's a quiet neuroscience truth here that's worth holding: When you bring mindful attention to sensation without panic, you are already changing the system. You are giving your brain new input. You are interrupting the automatic loop that says, "Sensation equals danger."

Notice also helps you separate signal from story. The story can run wild. Sensation tends to be more honest. It gives you a cleaner starting point.

Need

Need is the most important step, because it turns insight into support.

Once you've named the emotion and noticed the sensation, you ask one practical question: "What does my nervous system need right now?"

Sometimes it needs steadiness: a longer exhale, a grounded posture, less urgency, fewer words. Or perhaps it needs containment: a pause, space, a boundary, a moment to come down before you respond. It might need connection: a supportive person, a calmer tone, a repair, a reminder that you're not alone and not in trouble. Sometimes it needs action: not reactive action but aligned action. A boundary, a decision, a step that reduces the underlying stressor. And finally, it might need rest: food, sleep, water, a reduction in stimulation. Because the emotion isn't a deep psychological mystery; it's your biology asking for basic care.

Need is where people often get stuck because they skip straight to solving the external problem. They try to fix the email, fix the conflict, fix the child, fix the situation. But if the nervous system is still activated, fixing rarely feels like it's working. So this is where you practice supporting the system first, so the support becomes the foundation for whatever you do next.

How It Looks in the Moment

Imagine you feel a spike of anger. You can sense yourself sharpening, about to say something that will land like a weapon.

> Name: "This is anger."
> Notice: "Heat in my chest, jaw tight, breath shallow."
> Need: "I need to slow down and reduce
> intensity before I speak."

That might mean one longer exhale, followed by lowering your shoulders. Then saying, "Give me a second," and perhaps stepping away for a minute, not to avoid the conversation but to protect the relationship.

Or imagine anxiety arrives as urgency and mental rehearsal.

Name: "This is anxiety."
Notice: "Fast thoughts, tight stomach, scanning."
Need: "I need reassurance through the
body, not more thinking."

That might mean grounding through your feet, letting your eyes move around the room, lengthening the exhale, doing one small practical thing, and then pausing instead of spiraling.

Or imagine sadness arrives, and you immediately start trying to be productive to outrun it.

Name: "This is sadness."
Notice: "Heavy chest, lump in throat."
Need: "I need softness, not strategy."

That might mean giving yourself permission to feel it for two minutes instead of pushing it away. Reaching out to someone steady or letting yourself cry. Sometimes sadness completes when it's allowed to exist without being treated as an emergency.

What This Practice Builds Over Time

The goal isn't to do this perfectly. The goal is to become someone your nervous system trusts.

Each time you respond to an emotion with naming rather than shame, with noticing rather than avoidance, with need rather than self-attack, you create evidence that you are safe with yourself and that feelings don't have to become emergencies to be taken seriously.

Over time, that evidence changes the system. You stay connected, you recover faster, and you make fewer regrettable choices from a threatened state.

This is what emotional regulation looks like when it's real. Not a performance or a personality trait. Rather, a relationship with your own signals, built through repetition, kindness, and practice in ordinary moments.

And that, quietly, is how calm becomes a skill.

CLOSING: CALM IS STAYING CONNECTED TO YOURSELF

If you've had a complicated relationship with emotions, it makes sense.

Most people were never taught what emotions actually are. They were taught to manage appearances, to be "fine" and productive and pleasant, and to push through. And when emotions didn't cooperate, they were treated as problems to control or evidence that something was wrong.

But emotions are not the enemy. They're signals from a system that is trying to protect you, guide you, and keep you connected to what matters.

What engenders calm isn't learning to feel less. It's learning to understand what you feel and to meet it earlier, at the level it begins.

When you start noticing the body shift before the story hardens around it, you stop being blindsided so often. When you understand that your nervous system is scanning in the background, you stop making every surge a personal failure. When you approach emotions with curiosity instead of criticism, the system becomes less defensive. And when you practice Name, Notice, Need, you give your body something it can actually use: orientation, contact, and support.

You won't do this perfectly. Nobody does. There will be days when you notice late. Days when the story runs ahead. Days when you react and then realize afterward what was happening. That's not failure. That's being human in a nervous system that has learned patterns over time.

The win is that you can come back.

You can return to the signal. You can offer your system steadiness. You can repair when needed. You can learn your own patterns without turning them into a verdict on your character.

And as that becomes familiar, something subtle shifts. The emotions that arrive become part of your internal data, rather than a crisis to manage. Because calm isn't the absence of feeling. Calm is the ability to stay connected to yourself while you feel and to choose what comes next.

Chapter 4

YOUR NERVOUS SYSTEM—THE HIDDEN ENGINE BEHIND EVERY REACTION

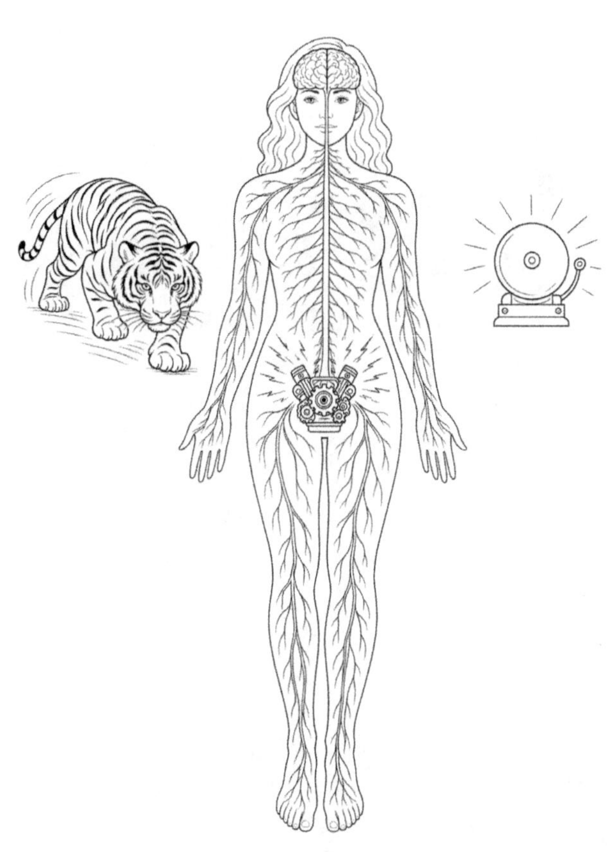

Why Calm Isn't Just a Mindset but Biology

You can't think your way into calm. If you could, none of us would spiral at 2 a.m. because someone read a message and didn't respond, snap at the people we love after a long day, or feel our whole body tense over a tone that wasn't even particularly sharp.

And yet many of us still try to logic our way through moments that are not logical at all.

Here's the truth I wish someone had told me decades ago: You don't feel overwhelmed because you're weak. You feel overwhelmed because your nervous system is overwhelmed.

Your mind follows your biology. Reactions don't start in your thoughts; they start in your body. If you've ever found yourself saying, "I know better, I just can't do better," this is why. Your survival brain and nervous system have already sprinted ahead, and the CEO is left trying to catch up.

This chapter is here to make the hidden engine inside you visible: the wiring that decides how safe you feel, how quickly you react, how long you stay activated, and how easily you return to steady.

Once you understand your nervous system, you finally understand yourself.

PART 1: YOUR NERVOUS SYSTEM ISN'T JUDGING YOU, IT'S PROTECTING YOU

Your nervous system is constantly running a real-time safety assessment in the background. Not as a moral judgement. Not to sabotage you. To protect you.

In this chapter, we're going to stop arguing with your reactions and start mapping the state they're coming from. Because the same email, the same comment, the same conversation can land completely differently depending on whether you're in Green, Yellow, or Red.

Once you can name the state, you can choose the right tool. Then calm stops being a personality trait and becomes a skill you can practice on purpose.

PART 2: THE THREE STATES OF YOUR BODY, AND HOW THEY SHAPE YOUR DAY

Most people treat emotions as unpredictable waves that crash in uninvited. But what shapes your emotional landscape, often more than your thoughts, intentions, or willpower, is your physiological state.

Your nervous system moves through different modes depending on whether it senses safety, possible threat, or danger. Your brain doesn't create these states so much as interpret them. Thoughts often arrive as stories that try to explain the body's state.

So, a more useful question than "What's wrong with me?" is "What state am I in right now?" To make this easier to recognize, we'll use a simple metaphor: a traffic light. Your nervous system signals when to go, when to slow down, and when to stop.

Green: Safe and Social

Green is your regulated state, the version of you that feels most like you. In Green, the parasympathetic system supports rest and digestion, and it also supports curiosity, learning, empathy, patience, connection, and perspective. Your prefrontal cortex is online, which means you can reflect, choose, and respond with nuance.

In this state, your body feels more open. Breath expands without your forcing it. Muscles soften. Heart rate steadies. Awareness widens. Green isn't the absence of challenge; it's the presence of capacity. You can disagree without disconnecting, set a boundary without it feeling like a battle, and make a mistake without spiraling into shame.

A real moment in Green: You and your partner disagree about something minor. There's tension, but you're not bracing. You stay present and curious. You can still feel connected, even while you're not aligned.

Yellow: Alert and Mobilized

Yellow is the nervous system's heads-up mode. Sympathetic activation begins to rise. Yellow isn't dangerous; it's adaptive.

It's the energy you use to meet deadlines, concentrate, get out the door on time, and respond to the practical demands of life.

In Yellow, you feel yourself lean forward internally. Breath shortens slightly. Shoulders lift. Attention narrows. You're a little more tense, a little quicker to irritation, a little more reactive. Yellow becomes a problem when it becomes baseline, when you're living in constant readiness, always anticipating, always bracing, never truly landing.

A real moment in Yellow: You drive home after a long day, hit one more red light, and irritation spikes. The light isn't the crisis. Your system has been on for hours, and this small inconvenience lands in a body that's already tense.

RED: FIGHT, FLIGHT, FREEZE, OR FAWN

Red is full survival mode, the body's emergency protocol. Adrenaline rises. Access to the prefrontal cortex reduces. The survival brain takes the steering wheel with dramatic confidence and zero nuance.

Red can feel like losing yourself. Heat rises, breath turns shallow, vision narrows, muscles brace, thoughts disappear, emotions intensify. From the outside, it may look like overreacting. From the inside, it can feel like drowning.

In Red, your body isn't misbehaving. It's sending a clear message: I don't feel safe. And once Red is running, logic won't bring you back. You don't think your way out of Red. You regulate your way out of Red.

Real moments in Red can look like snapping before you can think, going blank in a meeting, being flooded with shame at an eye roll, or feeling panic when plans change suddenly. These aren't personality flaws. They're survival responses. Red shows up when your system believes protection matters more than connection.

The Most Important Thing to Understand About States

Two truths change how you understand yourself. First, calm, clarity, empathy, and perspective are far more available when your nervous system senses safety. Second, you don't choose your state by willpower alone. Your nervous system shifts state based on cues.

So the work isn't to judge your state. It's to notice it, understand it, and learn how to shift it. That's where the skill begins.

Part 3: Your Body Is a Threat-Detecting Machine

As discussed in Chapter 3, **neuroception** is your system's automatic, lightning-fast assessment of safety. It draws on three streams of information. It reads the world around you. It reads what is happening inside your body (interoception). And it compares both to what your past has taught you to expect.

Moment by moment, the nervous system is asking a simple question: "Am I safe right now?" If the answer is yes, you tend to stay in Green. If the answer is uncertain, you drift toward Yellow. If the answer is no, you drop toward Red.

External Cues: What the World Feels Like

Your nervous system pays attention to details you don't always consciously notice. A sigh. A clipped tone. A shift in posture. A pause that lasts a beat too long. A raised eyebrow. The space between you and another person. The energy of the room you've just entered. All of that is processed before your thinking brain has finished interpreting it.

That's why the words "I'm fine" delivered with tight shoulders and a hollow voice can send your stomach into freefall. Your system isn't listening to the content. It's listening to the signal. It hears the emotional fingerprint, not the sentence.

Internal Cues: What Your Body Feels Like Inside

This is the part that surprises a lot of people because most of us have been trained to scan the world, not ourselves. But your nervous system is constantly registering signals such as heart rate, breath, muscle tension, temperature, gut sensations, and posture. Those signals don't sit in your body as neutral facts. They get interpreted. Your brain uses them to make fast predictions about what's going on and what you might need to do next.

Here's the catch. The brain prioritizes speed over accuracy. It doesn't wait to gather evidence and build a careful case. It reads sensation and moves quickly to meaning. A racing heart can be interpreted as anxiety. A sinking feeling can be interpreted as danger. Shallow breathing can be interpreted as "I'm not safe." Tight muscles can be interpreted as "I need to brace." Sometimes that interpretation is spot on. Other times, the sensation has a completely ordinary explanation, but the nervous system still treats it as a warning signal.

Your heart might be racing because you've had two coffees and skipped lunch. Your stomach might drop because your blood sugar is low, not because something terrible is happening. Your breath might be shallow because you've been hunched over your laptop for three hours. Your shoulders might be tight because you've been holding tension all day without realizing it. The nervous system doesn't care why the sensation is there. It cares that the sensation is there, and it uses it as part of its threat calculation.

This is why internal cues can create a loop. When something feels "off" in your body, your system starts preparing for danger, even if the original cause is harmless. Then the preparation itself becomes more evidence. The body gets more activated, which makes the mind search harder for a reason, which adds more threat, which creates more activation. You end up with a nervous system that is reacting to its own alarm.

Historical Cues: What Your Past Still Feels Like

Not all cues come from the present.

Sometimes your nervous system reacts hard because what's happening now resembles something that used to be.

This is one of the most important things to understand about the way the brain works. The nervous system is not designed to assess your current life with perfect accuracy. It's designed to keep you safe based on patterns. It uses memory and prediction to decide what to do next, and it does that quickly, often before conscious thought has caught up.

That's the point of learning. If you touched a hot stove once, you don't need a second experiment. Your system stores the pattern and protects you in the future. The problem is that humans don't just learn from stoves. We learn from relationships. From tone. From how conflict played out. From whether mistakes were safe. From what happened when we needed something. From whether people stayed close or withdrew.

Those patterns don't always get stored as neat, verbal memories. Often they're stored as expectations in the body. A kind of "when this happens, brace." A template that can run without you consciously agreeing to it.

Here is a useful way to think about this. Your nervous system is always asking, "What tends to happen next?"

If "next" used to be criticism, your body prepares for criticism.

If "next" used to be disconnection, your body prepares for disconnection.

If "next" used to be punishment, your body prepares for punishment.

If "next" used to be you having to manage someone else's emotions, your body prepares to manage.

And because this happens so fast, it can feel as though the emotion came out of nowhere. You can be in a perfectly ordinary moment and suddenly feel defensive, ashamed, panicked, or small. The present hasn't fully explained itself yet, but your body has already chosen a strategy.

This is also where the CEO/Caveman metaphor becomes more than a cute idea. The CEO wants nuance. The CEO wants evidence. The CEO wants to be fair. But the Caveman works on pattern. It asks, "Have we seen this before?" and if the answer is yes, it moves to protect you.

The important thing here is not to blame your history for everything. It's to stop pretending your nervous system has no history. You don't enter moments as a blank slate. You enter with learning, and that learning influences what your body predicts.

Once you understand that, you can approach these reactions differently. Instead of treating them as proof that something is wrong with you, you can treat them as the nervous system doing what it learned to do.

And that's where change becomes possible. When you can recognize a historical cue, you stop taking it as a full instruction. You still feel the activation, but you don't have to let the old template drive your next move. You can pause, steady your body, and gather more information. You can let the present reveal itself before you let the past write the ending.

The Big Takeaway About Threat Detection

Your nervous system isn't trying to ruin your life. It isn't trying to embarrass you or sabotage your relationships. It's trying to protect you, using the tools it has and the patterns it learned a long time ago.

And because that protective scanning happens so fast, it often gets there before your thinking mind does. This is why emotional regulation isn't about becoming "less reactive" through sheer willpower. It's about becoming more aware of the signals your body is using to make its safety decisions, and learning how to respond to those signals with skill rather than shame.

When you understand why your system reacts the way it does, the reactions stop feeling like personal failures. They start feeling like information. And information gives you options.

PART 4: WHY SOME PEOPLE STAY ACTIVATED ALL THE TIME

If you've ever thought, "Why do I react so strongly to tiny things? Why can't I handle what everyone else seems to handle?" there's something important to hear before you turn it into a character assessment.

Most of the time, this isn't overreacting. It's overload. And those two things are very different.

Your baseline matters. The stress, tension, vigilance, exhaustion, mental load, and emotional residue already in your system shape almost everything. A small stressor feels small when your baseline is low. The same stressor can feel catastrophic when your baseline is high because you're at capacity.

This is one of the most misunderstood things about stress: Your system doesn't reset every morning. It accumulates.

We talk about stress as if each day starts fresh, like waking up with a clean slate. Biologically, that isn't how it works. Your nervous system is more like a bucket. Everything you experience drips into it: poor sleep, skipped meals, rushing, conflict you didn't have the bandwidth to resolve, sensory overload, hormonal shifts, caffeine jolts, decision fatigue, emotional labor, the conversations you're avoiding, the people you're worrying about, and the mental load you're quietly carrying for everyone around you.

Individually, most of those things feel manageable. Collectively, they fill your bucket to the brim.

And when the bucket is already full, it doesn't take much to spill over. Most adults are walking around with their bucket already dangerously full, then punishing themselves when the smallest splash makes water go everywhere. But the problem isn't the splash. It's how full the bucket already was.

Nobody teaches us to think in terms of capacity. We're raised to believe we should "handle things better," as though handling is a personality trait rather than a physiological resource. Your nervous system doesn't care about should. It cares about load. When your system is full, almost anything can push it into activation.

Chronic stress rewires your baseline.

When your system is activated frequently (rushing, juggling, anticipating, firefighting), your nervous system adapts. It starts treating that heightened state as normal. Instead of returning to regulation after each stressor, your baseline shifts upward and settles closer to activation.

You're not panicked. You're braced.

You're subtly "on" all the time.

This can look like startling easily, tensing in conversations, catastrophizing neutral moments, getting irritated by tiny things, and losing patience more quickly than you want to. Sometimes it shows up in a different way: Rest feels uncomfortable, because stillness gives your body space to feel what it's been carrying.

It isn't that you're "an anxious person." It's that your nervous system has learned that vigilance equals safety, so it stays vigilant.

From a brain perspective, this makes sense. Under ongoing stress, the amygdala becomes more sensitive to threat cues, and the prefrontal cortex (the CEO) has a harder time doing its calm, integrative work. Tension becomes a default setting. Attention scans more often. Capacity to recover shrinks.

A stressed system narrows your window of tolerance.

There's a useful image here, even if it's not the main metaphor. Think of your capacity as a window.

When you're regulated, your window is wider. You can tolerate uncertainty, discomfort, stimulation, conversation, or minor conflict without being knocked off course. You still feel things, but you can stay connected to yourself while you feel them.

When you're depleted or carrying too much load, the window narrows. Everyday moments start to feel like too much. A simple question can land like criticism. Silence can feel like rejection. Minor conflict feels threatening. A change of plans feels destabilizing. A request feels overwhelming. A small mess feels like failure.

Nothing about the external world changed. Your capacity changed.

And when capacity shrinks, everything starts to feel personal.

The Hazards of Overload

Overload not only amplifies threat detection; it also alters cognition.

The CEO gets less influence. Working memory shrinks. Perspective narrows to the immediate moment. Problem-solving collapses into urgency. You can know intellectually that you're overreacting and still feel unable to stop because calm thinking becomes less accessible when the body is running in protection mode.

That's why people say, "I can't think straight," or "Everything feels urgent," or "I'm tired of being tired." It isn't a mindset failure. It's a state. When your nervous system is overloaded, your brain has less access to the functions that make you feel like you.

The Reframe That Changes Everything

If there's one truth worth taking from this, it's this: You don't need more willpower. You need more capacity.

Your nervous system isn't misbehaving. It's doing exactly what it was designed to do when it's running on fumes. Calm doesn't come from trying harder. Calm comes from having more room in your system and more room in your life.

Room to breathe. Room to reset. Room to return.

When your baseline lowers, so many things become easier. Patience comes back. Communication gets cleaner. Boundaries feel simpler. Tolerance expands. Your mind becomes available again.

Calm isn't something you force. It's what your body does naturally when it finally has enough space.

Part 5: The Hijack (When Biology Takes the Wheel)

A hijack isn't the moment you "lose it." It's the moment your biology takes command.

What you experience as snapping, shutting down, freezing, spiraling, or disappearing isn't a personal weakness. It's the survival sequence your nervous system was designed to run when it senses danger. If you've ever thought, "Why do I do this? Why can't I stop myself?" this is the answer.

There's relief in understanding the sequence. It doesn't excuse the behavior, but it removes the shame layer. You're not broken. You're predictable. In fact, you're beautifully, biologically predictable.

The whole cascade can unfold so fast you barely register the first beat before you're already in the middle of it. But when you slow it down, the pattern is remarkably consistent.

What Actually Happens in a Hijack

It starts with a cue, often a small one. A tone of voice. A glance. A message that says, "Can we talk?" Someone going quiet. A raised eyebrow. Being interrupted. A sudden noise. Sometimes the cue isn't in the room at all. It's a memory that flickers through or a story your mind writes in half a second.

Most of the time, you don't consciously notice the cue. You feel it. Your stomach flips. Your breath shortens. Your shoulders tense. Something in you braces, and that bracing is the match being struck.

Then the amygdala (your brain's threat detector) fires before you've had time to reason. It doesn't analyze nuance. It doesn't check whether the danger is physical, social, or emotional. It works by pattern recognition: This feels like something that once hurt me. And it fires quickly because, from an evolutionary standpoint, speed is safety.

This is often the moment you feel the rush: heat rising, tightness gathering, pressure building in your chest. People think this is the emotion itself, but it's more accurate to call it what it is. It's your body preparing for survival.

Once the threat system is engaged, chemistry follows. Adrenaline arrives first, spiking heart rate, sharpening senses, tightening muscles, and quickening breath. Cortisol follows to keep you alert and vigilant. Digestion slows. Blood flow shifts toward the limbs. Your whole body becomes primed to act.

That's why people say, "I felt myself switch." They did. A biological switch flipped.

Now comes the part that makes people feel most helpless. The prefrontal cortex (the CEO) starts losing influence. This is the part of your brain responsible for perspective, language, empathy, planning, and keeping your response aligned with your values. In perceived danger, the brain deliberately down-regulates it because thinking can slow you down. Reflection can delay action. Nuance can get you hurt.

So the system chooses speed over wisdom.

This is why, in the middle of activation, you might struggle to find words, forget what you were going to say, lose perspective, or feel your mind go blank. It's why it can feel impossible to "snap out of it," no matter how hard you try. The CEO hasn't disappeared because you're being dramatic. It has stepped back because your body believes the moment requires survival, not strategy.

With the CEO quieter, the Caveman brain takes over. The more ancient survival networks in your brain move to the front and start directing the scene. They don't speak fluent logic. They speak instinct. And they tend to choose from a small set of protective strategies: fight, flight, freeze, or fawn.

At this point, behavior is being driven by circuitry more than conscious choice. You're not choosing the reaction. You're experiencing it.

Then the peak passes. Adrenaline burns off. Cortisol settles. The CEO returns.

And this is where the second wave often hits.

With clarity comes replay. With replay comes judgment. I shouldn't have said that. Why did I react like that? I know better. I don't want to be this version of myself.

Here is the truth you need to hold gently: You didn't have full access to "better" in the moment. The CEO wasn't fully online. It wasn't available in the way you wish it had been. You were running a survival script.

This is also why shame is such a problem. Shame assigns moral meaning to a mechanical process. And shame doesn't prevent future hijacks. Shame fuels them because shame is registered as threat, and threat keeps the nervous system braced.

A Real-Life Example: The Interrupted Idea

You're in a meeting. You finally speak up, and you've been holding an idea you're proud of. Halfway through your sentence, someone interrupts you.

Your body reacts before your mind can explain it. The stomach drop. The rush. The subtle flush of heat. Your words vanish. Your attention narrows. You freeze, or you shrink back into silence. The self-criticism arrives so quickly that it feels like it was waiting for you.

Later, when you're alone, the replay starts. *Why didn't I say something? I sounded weak.*

But freezing in that moment isn't evidence of timidity. It's evidence of a nervous system that detected threat based on old learning. Maybe you were dismissed often. Maybe being talked over used to mean you weren't safe to take up space. Maybe staying small used to be the better strategy.

The hijack makes sense. And when reactions make sense, they become workable.

The Humane Reframe

A hijack isn't you failing. It's you surviving.

The more clearly you understand this sequence, the more power you gain. Not by forcing yourself to "stop overreacting" but by recognizing early cues and supporting your system before the cascade takes over.

You can't override biology. But you can work with it. You can learn the first signals that your system is tipping. You can respond earlier. You can guide yourself back toward connection, where calm thinking becomes available again.

You're not trying to wrestle your nervous system into submission. You're learning how to work with it, so protection mode doesn't have to become your default setting.

PART 6: PROTECTION MODE VS. CONNECTION MODE – WHY CALM IS A STATE, NOT A STRATEGY

Here's one of the most useful things you can learn about your nervous system.

In any given moment, it tends to prioritize one of two programs: protection or connection.

That doesn't mean life becomes neatly divided into "safe" days and "stressful" days. It means that in the moments that matter, your system generally chooses one job at a time. Either it is scanning for threat and preparing you to survive, or it is settled enough to connect, think clearly, and stay open.

This distinction explains so much of what people call "overreacting."

PROTECTION MODE: YOUR SURVIVAL SYSTEM IN ACTION

When your nervous system senses danger (physical threat or social threat), it activates the sympathetic branch of your nervous system. This is the mobilizing system built for quick reactions. You can think of it like an internal security guard: scanning, vigilant, ready to pull the alarm at the first sign of trouble.

When danger is real, this is exactly what you want. If your child runs toward the road, you don't want slow reflection. If a car stops suddenly in front of you, you don't want nuance. You want speed.

The problem is that protection mode doesn't only respond to cars and roads. In adult life, it can be triggered by tone, silence, a glance, a delayed reply, a disagreement, or a moment of uncertainty. And in protection mode, you don't respond from values. You react from wiring.

That explains why a conversation can fall apart the moment you feel criticized. Why conflict can make your mind go blank. Why empathy disappears when you feel attacked, why listening becomes hard when you're overwhelmed, and why patience evaporates when you're running on a thin buffer.

None of that is a personality flaw or a maturity issue, and it isn't fixed by simply "trying harder."

It's a state shift. When your system moves from connection to protection, the rules change.

Connection Mode: Where Calm Thinking and Relationship Live

Connection mode is different. It's slower, steadier, more spacious. This is the state where you feel grounded enough to be present and safe enough to stay open.

In polyvagal terms, this is supported by the ventral vagal branch of your parasympathetic nervous system. You don't need to memorize these terms. The idea is simple: Humans have built-in "safe and social" circuitry. When it's active, your face softens, your breath deepens, your voice becomes warmer, and your body becomes less braced. You can listen without defensiveness. You can speak without fear. You can tolerate nuance. You can repair after conflict. You can choose your response instead of being swept away by it.

This is the version of you your relationships recognize. The version that parents with more patience, partners with more steadiness, and leads with more clarity. It isn't perfect. It's simply the version of you that has access to your full range.

And here's the part the modern mind often resists at first: You cannot access connection mode until your body believes you're safe.

No amount of logic, affirmations, emotional intelligence, or communication tools can pull you fully into connection while your nervous system is still in protection. Calm is not a thought. It's a biological state. Thinking can support it, but thinking can't replace it.

WHY DISCONNECTION CAN FEEL LIKE DANGER

Polyvagal theory is useful here because it explains why connection isn't a nice extra. It's a nervous system requirement.

Alongside the ventral vagal "safe and social" pathway, there is another parasympathetic pathway often described as dorsal vagal shutdown. This is the system that can pull you toward collapse when something feels too much for too long, or when the body feels trapped, defeated, or out of options. It can show up as numbness, exhaustion, dissociation, or that heavy, internal "I can't."

Between connection and shutdown sits sympathetic activation: mobilization. It's where anxiety, urgency, irritability, and bracing live. You've already seen how easily that state can build if the system doesn't get enough recovery.

What matters is the direction. When you feel supported and safe, connection becomes easier to access. When you feel judged, uncertain, overwhelmed, or threatened, protection rises. When the system feels stuck or hopeless, shutdown can take over. None of this is drama. It's your nervous system doing what it does.

Real-Life Examples: Same Event, Different State

You send a message. They read it. Then nothing.

If you're in connection mode, your mind tends to land on the most grounded interpretation: They're probably busy. Your body stays relatively settled, and the situation remains a question, not a crisis.

If you're in protection mode, the meaning shifts instantly: What did I do wrong? Are they upset? Am I being ignored? Same event, two completely different experiences.

Your thoughts didn't choose the meaning first. Your state did.

Or take this: Your partner says, "We need to talk."

Connection mode hears, "Let's work through something together."

Protection mode hears, "Something bad is coming."

Again, nothing about your personality changed between interpretations. Your nervous system did.

Why This Matters for Calm

Calm isn't just the absence of conflict or the ability to look composed. Calm is the biological state from which clarity, empathy, patience, and connection are even possible.

When you're in protection mode, the goal is not to communicate better. The goal is to regulate first because regulation is what makes good communication available. You can only reliably choose your reactions when your nervous system is in connection mode. Everywhere else, biology tends to choose for you.

This isn't a personal flaw. It's design.

And the moment you can recognize which mode you're in, something softens. You stop fighting yourself. You stop demanding calm from a system that can't deliver it yet. You stop turning activation into a verdict.

Instead, you start working with your biology. You learn how to guide yourself back toward connection, where calm, clarity, and choice live.

Part 7: Regulating Your System – How You Actually Shift Back to Calm

Most people think regulation is the same thing as relaxation. They picture candles, bubble baths, or repeating a mantra their nervous system doesn't believe.

But real regulation isn't about becoming peaceful. It's about helping your body stop sounding the alarm.

To shift state, it helps to understand one truth that changes how you approach everything: The body leads the mind. A threatened nervous system doesn't take its cues from logic. It takes its cues from sensation, rhythm, posture, breath, and connection. When the body feels unsafe, the brain looks for danger. When the body begins to settle, the brain becomes capable of a different story.

There are three ways your system gets the message that it can stand down. They work together, but they don't all work equally well in every state.

Body to Brain

This is usually the fastest place to start, because it speaks the language your nervous system already understands.

When you change your physiology, you send a message upward. It isn't a motivational message. It's a biological one: We are safe enough to stand down a notch.

The vagus nerve plays a big role here. It begins in the brainstem and runs through the face and throat, down through the heart and lungs, into the gut. It is part of your body's safety circuitry. When it receives cues of steadiness (slower rhythm, softer muscle tone, orienting to the environment), it helps shift the system toward regulation.

That's why physical actions that seem almost too small to matter can make a difference.

You're in a meeting, and someone questions you sharply. You feel the surge, the internal brace, the urge to defend. Instead of panicking, you soften your shoulders. You unclench your jaw. You let your breath slow by a fraction. From the outside, nothing dramatic happens, but inside, you've offered your nervous system clear evidence: If I can soften, I can't be in immediate danger. Your brain listens to evidence like that. The intensity lowers. The CEO has a better chance of staying nearby.

Or you're at home, and your teenager sighs dramatically and walks out of the room. Your stomach drops. Heat rises. The old pattern starts running. In that moment, you lengthen your exhale. A longer exhale activates settling pathways in the nervous system.

It's one of the cleanest "stand down" signals you can give because it changes rhythm in a way your body recognizes immediately.

Body-first support can be subtle enough that no one around you notices you're doing anything. You might press your feet gently into the ground and feel the steadiness of the floor. You might place a hand over your sternum and let your body register contact and support. You might turn your head and look slowly around the room, letting your eyes orient to what is actually here, which can be surprisingly regulating because it tells the nervous system you are not trapped. You might hum quietly in the car, or soften your tongue, or run cool water over your wrists. You might shake out your hands, not as a performance but as a way of letting mobilization energy move through rather than getting stuck.

These aren't self-care hacks. They are biological interventions. They are how you lower the alarm from the inside.

And this is why body-first regulation matters so much: It works even when your thoughts don't want to cooperate. It doesn't require you to believe anything. It only requires you to give your nervous system new evidence.

Brain to Body

Once you're out of full hijack mode and the CEO is at least partly back online, the mind can help again.

This is where language and meaning become useful, not to override the body but to organize what the body is already starting to settle. One of the simplest examples is naming what you're feeling. When you label an emotion, activity tends to shift away from threat networks and toward the prefrontal cortex. In plain language, naming can help the amygdala quiet down and bring more of your thinking brain back into the room.

From there, you can gently fact-check the story your mind is building. You can ask, "What is actually happening now, and what does this remind me of?" You can remind yourself that sensation is not an instruction. You can ground in the present through your senses, not to distract yourself but to give your brain real data.

Top-down tools can be powerful, but they have a limit. They tend to work best when activation is moderate, not extreme. When you're in high protection, thinking tools often feel like trying to negotiate with a smoke alarm. That's why the body-first pathway comes first.

Nervous System to Nervous System

This is the most underrated pathway, and the most human.

Before you ever regulated yourself, someone regulated you. A parent rocking you. A teacher speaking softly. A friend sitting beside you when you cried. Human nervous systems are built to stabilize in the presence of other steady systems. That isn't dependency. It's biology.

Tone of voice, facial expression, warmth in someone's eyes, the steadiness of their breath: these are cues your nervous system reads. Sometimes they settle you faster than any technique because your body believes them at a deeper level.

You come home buzzing from work, muscles tense, thoughts loud. Your partner gives you a long, grounded hug, and your whole body sighs. That sigh isn't a personality trait. It's physiology. Your system just received evidence, through contact and presence, that it is safe enough to soften.

Co-regulation can come from a friend's calm tone, a colleague who brings steadiness, a therapist's attuned presence, or even a pet pressed against your leg. You were never meant to calm yourself entirely alone. Learning to allow support doesn't make you weak. It brings you back to design.

PART 8: WHY SELF-REGULATION FEELS HARD – IT'S NOT YOU, IT'S YOUR WIRING

There's a particular kind of frustration that comes with nervous system work. You can recognize the pattern as it starts. You can almost watch yourself getting hooked, spiraling, shutting down, snapping, or disappearing behind your eyes. And even with all the insight in the world, even after years of reading or therapy or intention-setting, the moment can still take you.

Most people interpret that as failure.

But it's usually the opposite.

Your biology is doing what it was designed to do. Your nervous system wasn't built for serenity. It was built for survival. It interprets the world through patterns, sensations, and history, not through self-help language, not through your best intentions, and not through the person you're trying so hard to become.

Once you understand the "why" behind this, a lot of shame can fall away. You stop treating your nervous system like an enemy and start treating it like a system that learned to protect you early, then kept running those same protective strategies into adult life.

Your baseline was shaped before you had words.

Your nervous system began forming long before you could explain what you felt. Before you had context or could make sense of anything, your body was already learning: Is the world predictable? Are the people around me available? Does distress get soothed, ignored, punished, or mocked? Is tension temporary, or does it linger?

Those early answers didn't become conscious beliefs. They became body beliefs, patterns etched into your physiology. If the emotional climate around you was unpredictable, inconsistent, or tense, your body learned to brace. People around you were not necessarily "bad," but your nervous system adapted to the atmosphere in which it lived.

And here's what no one tells you clearly enough. You grew up, but your wiring didn't automatically update. Adults often judge themselves for reactions rooted in climates they never chose. When you understand that, compassion becomes easier, and change becomes more realistic.

Stress doesn't leave your body on its own. It stacks.

Your nervous system carries yesterday into today. It carries the week into the month. Sometimes it carries decades.

Unprocessed stress becomes tension you don't even notice until it's chronic. Avoided conflict becomes the knot in your stomach that never quite leaves. Decision fatigue becomes irritability. Sleep debt becomes emotional fragility. Too much responsibility becomes that background hum of overwhelm you can't fully explain.

In that state, it doesn't take much to tip you over. You're not "set off" by the small thing. The small thing lands in a system already saturated. Like one more drop in a glass that's already full, it's not the drop that's the problem. It's the load the glass was carrying before the drop arrived.

Modern life is mismatched with your biology.

Your nervous system evolved for a world with slower rhythms, more recovery, and fewer constant demands. Danger was occasional, and rest was built into the day. You weren't designed for relentless noise, endless notifications, artificial urgency, overstimulation, and a mental load that never clocks off.

And yet that's what most people are living in: work pressure, household logistics, social obligations, screens, comparison, and a steady stream of "small emergencies" that keep the system activated.

Your biology hasn't caught up. We expect nervous systems to stay calm while living lives that are fundamentally overwhelming to the wiring. It isn't a moral failing when your system heats up. It's a capacity issue. It's load.

You were taught to behave, not to regulate.

Most of us didn't grow up with real emotional education. We were taught how to act, not how to process. "Calm down." "Stop crying." "Don't make a scene." "You're fine."

Those aren't regulation tools. They're shutdown commands.

So many adults become highly skilled at masking emotions but not at moving through them. From childhood, they learn to push through, to perform competence, to look fine on the outside while feeling anything but. When they reach adulthood, they assume their struggle is a personal flaw, when the truth is simpler: No one handed them the manual.

Learning late doesn't mean learning wrong. It just means you're building a skill that should have been taught as standard.

In survival mode, your brain disables calm thinking.

This part is worth repeating because it changes how you interpret yourself. In perceived threat, the prefrontal cortex (the CEO) loses influence. That's the part of the brain that supports perspective, emotion regulation, clear communication, and choice.

It doesn't go quiet because you're weak. It goes quiet because your brain believes speed matters more than sophistication. Reactivity matters more than reflection. Instinct matters more than insight.

That's why people say, "I knew what to do, but I couldn't do it." Or, "I understood what was happening, but I still reacted." That isn't hypocrisy. It's state. You can't expect yourself to think like a CEO when your brain thinks it's outrunning a lion, even if the "lion" is a sigh, a text message, or an uncomfortable conversation.

The work you're doing here is not to become a person who never gets activated. It's to become a person who understands activation early, responds with skill, and builds a life that creates more capacity in the first place. Calm becomes more available when the system has room, recovery, and the kind of support that helps it trust the present.

Part 9: Building a Nervous System That Supports Calm

Calm isn't something you stumble into. It's something you train your body to recognize.

If your nervous system is the engine of your emotional life, then the habits, rhythms, and environments you live inside every day are the fuel lines. They shape your baseline. They influence how much buffer you have, how quickly you recover, and how easily your system tips into protection mode.

This is the part many people overlook because it isn't glamorous. It doesn't come with a cinematic breakthrough. It's the quiet, unglamorous reality that a regulated nervous system is built in ordinary moments, not only in crisis ones.

You don't teach calm in the middle of chaos. You teach calm through repetition. You create dozens of small experiences that communicate safety consistently enough that the body starts to believe you.

Returning in Micro-Moments

Most people imagine regulation as something you do "properly," once a day, or when things fall apart. A meditation session. A long walk. A deep breathing exercise. All of those can help, but baseline change happens in a simpler way.

It happens through micro-returns. The smallest possible signals of safety, repeated often.

A softened jaw. A slower exhale. Shoulders dropping a fraction. Belly unclenching. Feet pressing gently into the floor. Eyes widening to take in the room. These moments can feel too small to matter, which is why people dismiss them. But the nervous system doesn't change through one heroic intervention. It changes through thousands of small corrections.

Think of it like tapping the brakes on a long downhill drive. You don't slam the brake once and hope for the best. You keep correcting gently, early and often, so the system doesn't build to the point of losing control.

A real example is the moment before you walk into a meeting. You're late. Your heart is pounding. Your breath is high and shallow. You can carry that activation straight into the room, or you can take ten seconds to lengthen your exhale and drop your shoulders. Nothing dramatic. Just a signal. We're okay. And you enter as a slightly different version of yourself.

Those micro-moments don't look impressive. But they are training. And training is what rewires.

Lightening the Load Your System Is Carrying

It's hard to regulate a nervous system that is already saturated.

Most of the time, the system isn't reacting only to the moment in front of you. It's reacting to the accumulated weight of everything it hasn't had space to process. Poor sleep. Skipped meals. The argument you swallowed. The responsibility you're holding alone. The background anxiety you carry without even naming it. The cognitive load. The sensory noise. The constant decision-making.

Your nervous system doesn't "forget" those things. It holds them.

This is why the same event can feel manageable on a good day and catastrophic on a bad one. The event didn't change. Your capacity did.

Lowering the background load isn't glamorous work. It often looks like the basics: sleep, food, movement, fewer decisions, fewer open loops, clearer boundaries, asking for help, saying no sooner, building recovery into your week like scaffolding rather than treating rest as a reward you earn.

When the background load lowers, your baseline lowers with it. Your buffer returns. The same world becomes easier to live in.

Increasing Cues of Safety Around You

Your nervous system doesn't calm because life is easy. It calms because it feels safe.

And safety is not only a thought. It's a set of cues.

Your environment shapes your internal state far more than most people realize. Warm light, soft textures, predictable routines, gentle sounds, uncluttered spaces, familiar rhythms—these aren't just aesthetic preferences. They are biological signals that tell the nervous system it can soften.

You are a mammal. Your system evolved to read the world this way. Warmth meant survival. Predictability meant stability. Nature meant nourishment. Steadiness meant you could let your guard down. It makes sense that modern sensory chaos can keep the system braced, even when nothing is "wrong."

You can feel this in your body. Walk into a cluttered room and notice what happens. Then walk into a tidy, softly lit space and notice again. The to-do list didn't change. But your internal landscape did.

When your external world sends consistent cues of safety, your nervous system trusts that it can step out of protection mode, even briefly. And those brief moments add up.

The Simple Version

If this feels like a lot, it's because it is a lot to hold all at once. But the practice is not complicated.

Building a calmer nervous system isn't about mastering every technique. It's about choosing a handful of simple, reliable supports and repeating them until your body starts to trust them. Your nervous system doesn't need perfection. It needs consistency. It needs kindness. It needs proof you're paying attention.

When your body receives enough signals of safety (small, steady ones), calm stops being something you chase. It becomes something you return to.

Part 10: The Real Reason Calm Is a Skill, Not a Trait

By now, you can probably feel the shape of it. Calm has never been about personality. It isn't about being naturally chilled, innately serene, or born with the kind of temperament that glides through life.

Calm is what happens inside you when your nervous system trusts the moment you're in.

When your body believes you're safe, your mind becomes clearer. Your attention steadies. Your reactions soften. The CEO steps forward, and the Caveman brain can finally ease its grip. You don't force calm; safety creates the conditions where calm becomes possible.

So the goal isn't to "be calm" as an identity. The goal is to become someone who returns more quickly and more reliably. Someone whose body doesn't stay braced as long. Someone who recovers faster after stress and comes back to themselves with less damage and less shame.

That shift has very little to do with temperament and everything to do with practice.

Calm isn't a gift some people received and others missed out on. It's a skill built through repetition, awareness, and gentleness. Every small moment of regulation teaches your body a new possibility. Every time you soothe instead of shame, you strengthen the pathway back. Every time you work with your system instead of fighting it, you make calm more familiar.

Not perfect. Not constant. Just more available. More reachable. More yours.

And once you start building buffer intentionally, something shifts. The same life events still happen, but you meet them from a different baseline. You have more range. More choice. More access to the part of you that can think, reflect, and respond.

That is where calm starts to become real.

Closing: You Were Meant to Learn Calm

Your nervous system isn't the problem. It's the pathway.

If there's one truth I want to leave you with at the end of this chapter, it's this: Your reactions make sense. Every one of them.

Your body has been trying to protect you in the only language it knows. Through tension and speed. Through bracing and shutting down. Through spiraling, defending, going quiet, going sharp. None of that means you're broken. It means you are wired for survival, and your nervous system has been doing its job.

You don't need to wrestle your biology into submission. You don't need to shame yourself into composure. You don't need to pretend you're fine when your body is telling you otherwise.

You need understanding, and you need partnership.

When you learn how your system works (cues, states, hijacks, patterns, and pathways), calm stops being something you chase from the outside. It becomes something you cultivate from the inside out. Not by forcing yourself to cope but by creating enough safety and capacity that coping becomes less necessary.

Before you move on, pause for a moment.

Take one slow breath. Let your shoulders drop slightly. Unclench your jaw, just a little. Give your body one small piece of evidence that, right now, it can soften.

You were never meant to "do calm" through willpower. You were meant to learn it.

And you already are.

Chapter 5

THE CALM GAP

CREATING SPACE BETWEEN TRIGGER AND REACTION

There's a moment most people never notice.

It happens before the snap, before the shutdown, before the email you wish you hadn't sent. It happens before the sharp words leave your mouth, or the familiar knot tightens in your chest and turns into a full internal storm.

It's brief, quiet, and easy to miss.

And once you learn to see it, everything changes. That moment doesn't make you magically calm, but it's the one occasion where your nervous system is still deciding what happens next.

That moment isn't just a pause. It's a doorway.

The Calm Gap is the signature move in this book because it works at the only point that actually changes outcomes: before the reaction becomes a habit in motion. It's not a mindset. It's not a personality upgrade. It's a timing intervention.

When people say, "I just need to be less reactive," they usually mean, "I need to stop doing the thing I do once I'm already flooded." But flooded brains don't negotiate. Flooded brains protect. The Calm Gap is where you catch the wave early enough to steer, even slightly, before it becomes a dump-truck of chemistry and regret.

Part 1: The Moment You've Been Missing

Most people believe their reactions are instant.

One moment they're fine, and the next they're overwhelmed, defensive, angry, withdrawn, spiraling. It can feel like there is no space in between, like calm disappears and chaos takes over in a single step.

But that's not actually what's happening.

Your nervous system doesn't flip a switch. It moves through a sequence. And hidden inside that sequence is what I call the Calm Gap, a tiny window between activation and action where choice becomes possible again.

Not because you suddenly became "better at self-control." Not because you fixed your personality. Simply because your biology gives you a sliver of room to interrupt the pattern, if you learn how to find it.

Picture something familiar.

It might be tiny. The moment you notice a breath change. The moment your throat tightens like you're about to defend yourself. The moment you feel that hot urgency to respond quickly, so you don't "lose" something.

The Calm Gap often feels like a flicker of choice that your system tries to skip past. It's the half-second where you could keep going on autopilot, or you could do one small thing that changes the ending.

You're in a conversation that suddenly shifts tone. A comment lands wrong. Someone's voice sharpens. An email feels loaded. Before you've had a chance to think it through, your body reacts. Your jaw tightens. Your chest contracts. Your stomach drops. Your thoughts speed up, or disappear entirely.

Then, almost automatically, you respond. You snap back, or you shut down. You over-explain, retreat, people-please. You fire off a message you immediately regret.

Later, you replay it all.

Why did I react like that? I knew better. I promised myself I wouldn't do that again.

And slowly, quietly, the old story creeps in: This is just how I am.

But here's the truth most people never get taught: The problem isn't that you have reactions. The problem is that they happen so fast, you don't get to participate.

Between the trigger and the reaction, there is always a moment.

It might be less than a second. It might show up as sensation rather than thought. It might feel more like urgency than awareness. But it's there.

That micro-pause is where your nervous system decides what happens next.

I call it the Calm Gap, not because you feel calm inside it (you usually don't), but because it's the only time calm can begin to be built. The Calm Gap isn't about stopping emotion. It isn't about "thinking positive" or talking yourself out of what you feel. It definitely isn't about responding perfectly.

It's simply this: a small window of time where your nervous system hasn't fully committed to the old reaction yet.

That's it. And that is enough.

Part 2: Why Willpower Fails and Timing Works

Most self-help advice aims at the end of the sequence.

It tells you to communicate better, regulate your emotions, choose healthier responses, pause and reflect. It's not wrong advice. It's just late-stage advice. It works best when your system is steady enough to think clearly, hold perspective, and choose your words.

But when your nervous system is already in motion, logic arrives late to the party.

This is partly about wiring speed. Threat pathways are designed to act fast because, in a real danger moment, speed is the point. Your thinking brain is powerful, but it's slower and more expensive. It needs oxygen, time, and a bit of internal steadiness.

So when your system detects threat, it doesn't wait for a board meeting. It moves first, explains later. Willpower fails when it's asked to do a job it wasn't designed to do: override survival chemistry already in progress.

By the time you're telling yourself to calm down, your body has often already made a decision: not safe, not settled, not okay.

The amygdala has flagged threat, stress chemistry has started moving through the system, and your access to the prefrontal cortex (the part that helps you reflect, regulate, and choose) begins to shrink.

That's why you can "know better" and still not be able to do better in the moment.

It isn't a character flaw. It's timing.

Willpower asks your CEO to take over after your Caveman brain has already pulled the alarm. It asks for discipline after the surge. It asks for rational choices while your body is already braced for impact.

And then, when it doesn't work, you conclude you must be weak, undisciplined, or "bad at regulation."

You're not. You're just intervening after the chemistry has already taken the wheel.

The Calm Gap works for a different reason. It shows up earlier. Earlier than the words. Earlier than the behavior. Earlier than the regret. It's the small moment where your system has been activated but hasn't fully committed to the old script yet.

And this is the part that surprises people: You do not need to feel calm to use the Calm Gap.

You don't need clarity. You don't need emotional insight. You don't need the perfect response. You just need a few seconds of interruption because those seconds change what's happening inside your body.

Sometimes the Calm Gap is literally three seconds.

Three seconds doesn't sound like much, but biologically, it's huge.

Here's a very normal modern-life version. You get an email from your boss that starts with, "Can you call me?" No context. Your stomach drops. Your mind starts drafting a resignation letter and an apology at the same time.

The Calm Gap is the three seconds where you don't reply from the spike. You don't send the panicked "Sure! Is everything okay??" You don't launch into ten explanations. You simply pause, soften your jaw, take one longer exhale, and decide to gather information before you generate a catastrophe.

That small pause doesn't make you calm. It makes you available. And availability is where better choices live.

At first, the Calm Gap can feel almost theoretical. People often say, "I don't have a gap," or "It happens too fast," or "I only realize after it's over."

That doesn't mean the gap isn't there. It usually means it's untrained.

Awareness comes before choice. Repetition comes before confidence. Once you start looking for the gap, you begin to notice it in subtle ways. Not as wisdom, more like early signals: the urge to speak sharply, the tightening before the shutdown, the spike of heat before the anger, the rush before the reassurance-seeking.

Those are not failures. They are information.

And early information is exactly where change becomes possible.

PART 3: WHAT THE CALM GAP ACTUALLY IS

To understand the Calm Gap, we need to clear up one deeply unhelpful assumption.

Most people believe reactions start in thoughts. The story goes something like this: I thought something, then I felt something, then I reacted.

That makes sense because thoughts are loud. They're the part you can hear.

But neurologically, it's not where the sequence begins.

Most reactions don't start in your mind. They start in your threat system. In the language we've been using, they start in the Caveman brain, the fast, protective part of you whose job is survival.

But here's the part that changes everything.

Your threat system does not usually go from zero to full tiger-mode in a single instant. There is a brief moment, sometimes only a few seconds, between the first signal of threat and the full survival response. A moment where your body has registered danger, but your system hasn't fully committed to the old script yet.

That moment is the Calm Gap.

It's the space where the Caveman has spotted the tiger but hasn't started running.

And crucially, that moment is biologically responsive.

Your body has a built-in braking system. When you send cues of safety through posture, breath, and slowing, you're applying the brake early enough that the threat response doesn't need to hit full volume.

This is why small physical shifts can have outsized effects. You're not "being dramatic" when a breath changes your entire state. You're using your biology the way it was designed to work.

Adrenaline spikes quickly, but it also responds quickly to new information. When you pause physically, even slightly, you send a different signal back through the system: We see it, and we're not moving yet. When you soften one piece of bracing, when you lengthen an exhale, when you ground your feet, you're not being "positive."

You're giving your nervous system evidence.

Evidence that the threat may not require immediate survival action.

That evidence slows escalation. It reduces intensity. It gives the CEO a chance to stay present or come back sooner.

You're not calming yourself down. You're buying time.

And time is what makes choice possible.

Part 4: Recognizing Your Early Signals – Meeting Your Caveman Before He Takes Over

If the Calm Gap is where change happens, your early signals are how you find the door.

Most people don't miss the gap because it isn't there. They miss it because they've been taught to look in the wrong place. They track thoughts, words, and behavior, but by then the system is already moving. The body has already started shifting state.

Early signals rarely show up as sentences. They show up as sensation.

Your threat system speaks in the language of the body, not in the language of insight. That's why reactions often feel physical before they feel emotional or cognitive. You don't usually think, "I'm about to get defensive." You feel it: tightening in the jaw, contraction in the chest, heat rising, clenching in the stomach.

Sometimes it's not even a clear sensation. It's an urge.

An urge to speak quickly. An urge to fix it. An urge to explain. An urge to shut down. An urge to escape the room, to check your phone, to tidy something, to do anything except stay with the discomfort that just arrived.

Those signals aren't random. They're your nervous system saying, "I've spotted something that looks like danger."

Most of us were trained to override these cues. We were taught to push through, stay composed, be professional, not make a fuss, keep going. So we learn to ignore the early signals and deal with the fallout later.

Recognizing early signals isn't about becoming more sensitive. It's about becoming more accurate.

And here's the reassuring part: Your early signals are usually consistent. They don't change much from one situation to the next. What changes is the story you attach to them.

Most people have a signature doorway. A predictable first clue that shows up again and again. For one person, it's tight shoulders and shallow breath. For another, it's heaviness in the chest and a subtle mental fog. For someone else, it's a rush of urgency: Respond now. Fix it now. Say something now.

You don't need to track everything. You only need to recognize the first signal. Learn the first breadcrumb your nervous system drops because that breadcrumb is where the Calm Gap opens.

One of the simplest ways to find it is to look at a reaction you didn't love and rewind the tape, just a few seconds. Not the whole event. Not the whole conversation. Just the beginning.

What did you notice first? Where did you feel it? What was the very first change?

Often, the answer isn't "I got angry." It's "My chest tightened," or "My throat closed," or "I felt urgency."

That's the Calm Gap opening.

Urgency matters because it's your threat system's favorite trick. Tigers required immediate action. Emails usually don't. Learning to notice urgency without obeying it is one of the fastest ways to widen the gap because it interrupts the illusion that this must be dealt with right now.

There's also a small paradox here: Sometimes noticing is the tool.

When you name a sensation internally, something can soften. You didn't analyze it, but you acknowledged it. It can be as simple as tight chest . . . heat . . . urgency. Short. Neutral. Factual.

That kind of noticing creates space all by itself.

Part 5: How to Widen the Calm Gap – Practical Tools for Real Life

Once you can recognize your early signals, the next question is obvious: Okay . . . now what?

This is where people assume they need control, perfection, or the perfect line.

They don't.

Widening the Calm Gap isn't about control. It's about delay. You're not trying to stop your threat system from reacting. You're slowing it down long enough for your thinking brain to join you.

That's the whole game.

Every tool that works here has the same purpose: buy a few seconds.

Not minutes. Not mastery. Seconds.

Because seconds can change chemistry. Seconds can soften intensity. Seconds can keep the CEO within reach. Seconds can be the difference between the old script and a slightly different first move.

The simplest place to start is the body because the body is where the Caveman speaks.

If you can soften one physical cue, you interrupt momentum. Unclench your jaw. Drop your shoulders. Put both feet on the ground. Let one slow exhale out through your mouth. None of this looks impressive, but your nervous system isn't impressed by impressive.

It's impressed by evidence.

A body that can soften is a body that isn't sprinting for its life.

Delay works the same way.

The Calm Gap is often protected by a sentence. Not a perfect sentence. A functional one. The kind you can use at work, at home, in conflict, and in parenting without needing a dramatic speech.

Think of it as buying time with dignity. You're not avoiding. You're regulating so you don't make it worse.

Urgency will insist you need to reply now, decide now, explain now, fix it now. Most of the time, you don't. Delay is regulation. Out loud, it can sound like, "Let me think about that," or "Can I get back to you?" or "I need a moment." Internally, it can be even simpler: I don't need to respond right now.

One longer exhale is another clean stand-down signal. You don't need a complicated technique. You just need to lengthen the out-breath slightly. Once is enough. Twice is a bonus. It tells your nervous system you're not in immediate danger, and that message travels faster than logic.

Then there's the tool that feels almost too small but is surprisingly powerful: naming without narrating.

When activation occurs, the mind wants to explain the sensation. Explanation pulls you into the story, and the story can pour petrol on the fire. Noticing keeps you in the space. Tight chest. Heat. Urgency. You're not analyzing yourself. You're registering what's happening.

And finally, widen the gap by changing the first move.

You don't need the perfect response. You just need to not do the automatic one.

If your pattern is snapping, soften your voice. If your pattern is shutting down, stay physically present a few seconds longer. If your pattern is over-explaining, say less. If your pattern is fleeing, pause before leaving.

A small deviation is often enough to disrupt the loop because it sends your nervous system a new kind of evidence: We have choices here.

This is what success looks like early on.

You still react, but less intensely. You pause and still say the thing, but differently. You notice after the fact, but sooner than before.

That counts.

Nervous systems learn through repetition, not perfection.

PART 6: WHAT HAPPENS WHEN YOU PRACTICE THE CALM GAP – HOW SMALL PAUSES CHANGE YOUR BASELINE

At first, the Calm Gap feels like something you do in a moment. A pause before you speak. A breath before you reply. A delay before you act.

It can feel almost too small to matter.

But beneath the surface, something important is happening.

Every time you widen the Calm Gap, your nervous system learns a new pattern. And nervous systems learn through experience, not intention. They don't update because you decided you wanted to be calmer. They update because you repeatedly give them evidence that a cue doesn't require an emergency response.

Most people assume their emotional baseline is just "how they are." Reactive. Sensitive. On edge. Tired. Wired.

But baseline isn't a personality trait. It's a trained state.

It reflects what your nervous system has come to expect from life: how often it needs to be alert, how quickly it should mobilize, how much danger it assumes is present in ordinary moments.

When stress has been chronic, the system adapts by staying ready. That readiness can show up as hypervigilance, irritability, emotional flatness, constant low-grade tension. Your nervous system has decided this is normal.

Each pause sends a new message: We can slow down here. We don't need to escalate. This is survivable.

Those messages don't land as affirmations. They land as physiology.

This is how your nervous system updates its predictions. It doesn't change because you understand a concept. It changes because it experiences a new ending often enough that the old ending stops feeling inevitable.

Every Calm Gap moment is a new data point: "We felt the spike, and we didn't have to sprint." Over time, your system starts expecting that you will pause. That expectation is what lowers your baseline. It's not magical. It's learned.

A slightly softer jaw. A longer exhale. A nervous system that stands down sooner than it would have last month. Over time, those small shifts add up.

You begin to recover faster after difficult moments. Your reactions soften. You don't replay things for as long. Your body settles sooner.

The Caveman learns that not every cue requires a sprint. And the CEO becomes easier to access.

Sometimes calm feels unfamiliar at first. If your system is used to activation, quiet can feel strange. You might notice restlessness, boredom, discomfort in stillness, even the urge to create urgency just to feel normal again.

That doesn't mean the work isn't working. It often means your nervous system is adjusting to a lower level of perceived threat.

One of the biggest outcomes of this practice isn't "staying calm." It's self-trust.

Each time you pause instead of reacting automatically, your system registers something simple and powerful: I can handle this. Not perfectly, not elegantly, but enough.

Over time, that trust compounds. You stop fearing your own reactions. You stop bracing for yourself. You begin to believe you'll find your way through moments, even messy ones.

Progress is quieter than people expect.

It often sounds like "I didn't spiral as long," or "I caught it sooner," or "I didn't make it worse."

Those are big wins.

Part 7: When the Calm Gap Feels Out of Reach – Repair, Not Perfection

There will be moments when everything you've read so far feels unavailable.

No pause. No space. No choice. Just reaction.

You snap. You shut down. You spiral. You say the thing you swore you wouldn't say again. And then the familiar voice arrives: I failed. What's the point? I should be better by now.

Those moments do not undo the work. They are part of it.

When activation is high enough, the threat system takes full control. This is more likely when stress has been chronic, when your system is overloaded, when a trigger hits an old wound, or when multiple pressures stack at once.

In those moments, your nervous system isn't choosing poorly. It's protecting aggressively.

When you can't access the Calm Gap before the reaction, the work moves after.

This is where repair matters.

Repair is not self-punishment. It's not endless replay. It's not promising yourself you'll "do better." Repair is what teaches your nervous system that even when things go sideways, you are still safe with yourself.

Repair can be simple. You notice what happened without judgment. You acknowledge activation. You help your body come down. You take responsibility without self-attack. You make a clean repair in the relationship if needed.

A clean repair can be unbelievably regulating for everyone involved. Something like "That came out sharper than I meant. I'm going to reset and try again," or "I'm activated. I care about this, and I want to come back when I can hear you properly."

Repair isn't a performance. It's leadership. It tells your nervous system, and often the other person's, "We can have activation without disconnection."

And one warning is worth being clear about: Self-criticism makes this harder. Shame keeps the nervous system in threat. It tells the Caveman, "I'm not safe, even with myself."

An unsafe system doesn't learn. It braces.

After a big reaction, the body often needs resolution before analysis. Sometimes that looks like a slow walk, stretching, shaking out your arms, a long exhale, or sitting quietly and letting the chemistry burn off.

This is not avoidance. It's helping your body complete the stress cycle so you can think again.

And here's the reframe that changes the emotional tone of the whole process: The Calm Gap can happen after the reaction, too.

It can look like apologizing. Repairing. Choosing not to spiral. Coming back to yourself instead of abandoning yourself.

Progress is measured by recovery, not avoidance.

PART 8: INTEGRATING THE CALM GAP INTO DAILY LIFE – FROM SKILL TO HABIT

At some point, you might wonder, "Am I supposed to do this all day? Pause before every email? Notice every sensation? Manage every reaction?"

No.

The Calm Gap doesn't become powerful through effort. It becomes powerful through integration.

It's not something you force into your life. It's something you learn to notice where it already exists, especially in ordinary transitions: before you open a message, between hearing something and responding, while you walk from one room to another, as you reach for your phone, in the space between finishing a task and starting the next.

If you want this skill to stick, practice where it's easiest first. Not in the biggest fight. Not in the deepest trigger. In the small, repeatable moments that happen every day.

Before you open your inbox. Before you walk into the house. Before you answer your phone. Before you respond to a message that has a weird tone. Those are "low-stakes reps." They train your system to pause automatically, so when the stakes are high, the pause is already familiar.

Your environment can do some of the work for you. External structure creates internal safety. Predictable routines, clearer start-and-stop points, fewer rushed transitions, and small moments of completion. These reduce the need for your system to stay on high alert.

And you don't need to practice the Calm Gap in every interaction.

One genuine pause, felt and honored, is enough to reinforce the pattern.

Your nervous system doesn't count reps. It learns from meaningful moments.

Over time, something subtle shifts. You stop bracing yourself. You start trusting that you'll notice sooner, pause when you can, and repair when you need to.

That trust creates space. And space is where calm begins.

CLOSING: THE SPACE THAT CHANGES EVERYTHING

If you take nothing else from this chapter, take this: You are not reacting because you lack self-control. You are reacting because your nervous system learned to move fast.

And speed can be retrained.

The Calm Gap isn't something you have to create from scratch. It's something you learn to notice, then return to. A doorway that was always there, waiting for a little attention.

You don't have to become a calmer person overnight. You don't have to catch every reaction or master every tool. Just keep returning to the pause, even when it's small, even when it comes late, even when all you can do is repair afterward.

Over time, those pauses teach your nervous system something it has been longing to learn: Not every cue is danger. Not every emotion requires action. Not every moment needs escalation.

And slowly, quietly, the Caveman starts looking to the CEO again. Not for control, but for perspective.

This is what calm looks like in real life. Not perfection. Space.

Space to choose, to recover, to trust yourself again.

Chapter 6

REGULATING IN REAL TIME

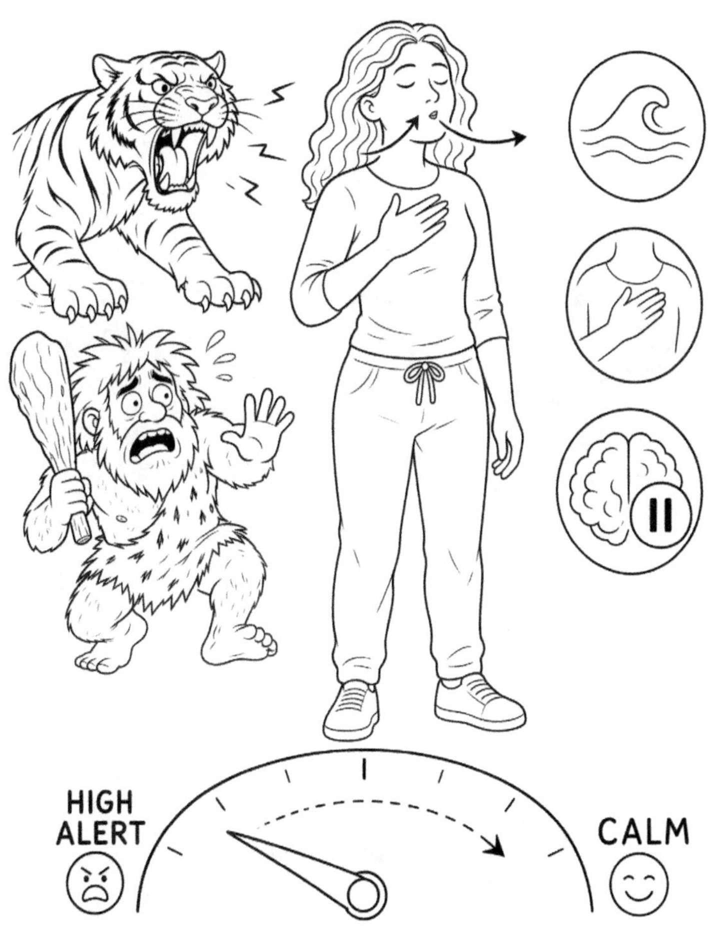

How to Shift State When You're Already Activated

Sometimes the pause doesn't arrive in time.

You notice yourself mid-reaction, already tight, already flooded. Your heart is racing. Your thoughts are either loud and fast, or they've vanished completely. The Calm Gap feels like it belongs to another version of you, the one who had time to think.

If that's been your experience, nothing has gone wrong.

It doesn't mean you missed your chance. It doesn't mean you're back at the start. It simply means your nervous system crossed a threshold, and once that happens, the work is different. Not harder, just different.

Sometimes you're already in it. You're already in the meeting where your mind goes blank. You're already in the argument where your body takes over. You're already in the parenting moment where you feel outmatched. You're already in the internal spiral that seems to arrive from nowhere.

The most important thing to understand is simple, and it can be deeply relieving: **When your nervous system is highly activated, thinking harder won't help.**

That's because activation reduces access to the prefrontal cortex (the part of your brain that helps you reason, reflect, find words, and take perspective). In other words, the CEO temporarily loses influence.

In those moments, it's not a lack of insight that gets you. It's timing. Your body moved first. This is where people often get stuck.

They know what they "should" do. They've read the advice. They've understood the patterns. But in the moment, none of that knowledge seems reachable. The words don't come. The insight disappears. The body surges or shuts down. Later, when the chemistry wears off, the self-judgment arrives and tries to make it mean something about who they are.

But this isn't a moral issue. It's a physiological one.

And once you understand that, something changes.

You stop trying to solve an activated state with thinking tools. You start working with your nervous system instead of fighting it.

That's the pivot.

When activation is high, you don't win by thinking harder. You win by supporting your state first. When the body stands down even slightly, the mind becomes available again.

Before you can reframe, before you can communicate clearly, before you can make grounded decisions, before you can "handle it better," your nervous system needs help settling, even a little. Not later, when the moment is over. Not only after you've escaped the situation. In real time, in the moment you're in, with the constraints you have.

That doesn't mean you need perfect conditions. It doesn't mean you need to leave the room, close your eyes, meditate for ten minutes, or take a walk you don't have time for.

It means you need the kind of support that works at the level of the body.

Because when the body begins to settle, the mind becomes available again.

One more clarification matters here, because people often misunderstand what regulation is.

Regulation is not relaxation. Regulation is simply helping your nervous system shift down a gear so you have more access to choice again.

Often, you don't need to get all the way back to calm in the middle of an intense moment. You just need to move away from the edge.

You don't need to return to Green in the middle of an intense moment. You just need to move away from Red.

And by the end of this chapter, I want you to feel one very specific thing: **Even when I'm already activated, I know what to do.**

That knowing changes how you show up. You're working with your biology instead of trying to outthink it.

PART 1: WHY THE RIGHT SUPPORT DEPENDS ON YOUR STATE

One of the biggest reasons people conclude that "regulation doesn't work" is that they try to reason with themselves when they're flooded. They try to talk it through when the body has already declared an emergency. They try to "calm down" using logic when their nervous system is in protection mode and logic is temporarily offline.

That mismatch creates frustration. It often creates shame. Why can't I make this work?

But the nervous system isn't one-size-fits-all. It doesn't operate as calm versus not calm. It moves through states, and each state needs a different kind of support.

A helpful way to picture this is as gears. In the brain, this "gear change" is partly about which networks are getting resources. When threat is perceived, survival circuitry gets louder, and the systems for language, perspective, and flexible thinking get quieter.

Sometimes you're steady and connected. You can think clearly. You can reflect. You can choose.

Sometimes you're mobilized. Your body is preparing for action. You feel urgency. You feel tension. You feel irritability or anxiety. Your attention narrows, and you want to fix things quickly. You are still present, but less spacious.

And sometimes you're in full survival mode. Your system has tipped into fight, flight, freeze, or fawn. Reaction is fast. Thinking becomes limited. Language can disappear. Your body is either flooded or shut down. The Caveman is in charge.

None of these states is bad. They are adaptive responses to what your nervous system believes is happening. The key is that different states require different interventions.

This is why thinking tools fail when you're in Red. When you're highly activated, your system is not interested in nuance, long-term planning, or insight. It is focused on immediate safety. Blood flow and neural resources shift toward the networks that support quick survival responses and away from the networks that support reflection and reasoning.

So when you try to reframe in Red, it can feel impossible. When you try to "communicate better," you may not be able to find words. When you try to talk yourself down, it may escalate the frustration because you're asking your brain to do something it can't fully do in that state. That doesn't mean you're resistant. It means your biology is prioritizing protection. In Red, the goal is not insight. The goal is stabilization.

Yellow is where real-time regulation has the most leverage. Yellow is the zone where you're activated but still reachable. There is still some awareness. There is still some access to choice. The CEO can still get a word in. A small body-based shift can change the trajectory quickly because your system hasn't fully tipped into survival.

And even if you are already in Red, the aim is the same. You are not trying to leap back to calm. You are simply trying to guide your system back toward Yellow. Not calm. Just less activated.

This is why regulation works best from the bottom up. When the body leads, the brain follows.

In high activation, the most effective support starts with sensation and rhythm. It starts with breath, posture, movement, and physical cues of safety. It starts with signals your nervous system can actually receive in the moment. Explanations can come later, when the system is ready.

And it's worth naming what this is not.

Regulating in real time is not about suppressing emotion, or forcing yourself to behave, or becoming numb, or pretending you're fine.

It's about giving your nervous system enough evidence to stand down so you can stay present and make choices that align with who you actually are.

Even partial signals help. A small shift counts. Because a small shift is often the difference between spiraling further and coming back sooner.

PART 2: HOW TO TELL WHAT STATE YOU'RE IN WITHOUT OVERTHINKING IT

Before you can support your nervous system, you have to know what it's doing.

Not in a perfect, clinical way. You're not trying to diagnose yourself. You're simply trying to answer one practical question in real time: "What kind of support do I need right now?"

That question only makes sense if you can recognize your state.

And here's the good news: You don't need to be highly self-aware to do this. You don't need to sit quietly and analyze your feelings.

You don't need to label the emotion correctly or work out where it came from.

Your body will tell you.

State shows up first as sensation: speed and tension and breath and posture. It shows up in what your attention does. It shows up in what becomes easy and what becomes hard.

Most people miss it because they've learned to override it. They've learned to keep functioning through the signals, which means the signals have become background noise.

Part of building calm as a skill is learning to bring those signals back into the foreground, gently and without drama. A simple way to start is to notice what changes in three places: the body, the mind, and your behavior.

When You Are Steady

When you are steady, your body tends to feel more open. Your breath is deeper without you forcing it. Your shoulders are not trying to become earrings. Your jaw isn't clenched. There's some softness in your belly. Your eyes and attention can move around without feeling trapped. You might still be busy, but you are not bracing.

Your mind feels more spacious in this state. You can take perspective. You can think about tomorrow without panic. You can tolerate uncertainty. You can hold two truths at once. You can feel something without immediately needing to fix it.

And your behavior reflects that. You respond rather than react. You can listen. You can pause. You can choose your words. You can stay connected to the person in front of you, even if you don't agree with them.

This is the state we often call "calm," but it's more accurate to call it regulated. It's Green. It doesn't mean life is perfect. It means your nervous system is not in protection mode.

When You Move into Activation

When you move into activation, you'll often feel it in your body first.

Your breath gets shallower or higher in the chest. Your muscles tighten. Your jaw or shoulders take on more load. Your heart rate increases. You might feel heat in your face or chest. You might feel restless energy in your hands or legs, like you need to do something.

In this state, your mind starts to narrow. You become more focused on what's wrong, what needs fixing, what could go wrong. Your thoughts might speed up. You might find yourself looping. You might feel less patient, more urgent, more reactive.

It can also show up as a sense of "I have to handle this right now," even when the situation doesn't actually require immediate action.

Behaviorally, this is the state where you start moving faster. You interrupt more. You multitask. You become more controlling, or you withdraw slightly. You might find yourself doing things to reduce discomfort quickly, even if they don't actually help long-term.

This is Yellow. It's activation. It is not failure. It's a normal nervous system response to demand.

Yellow is also the state where regulation has the most power, because you still have access to choice. You may not feel calm, but you are still reachable. You can still shift.

When You Cross into a Higher Level of Activation

When you cross into a higher level of activation, things change more noticeably. This is the state where your nervous system has decided, consciously or not, that something is unsafe or overwhelming. Your body shifts into protection mode.

Sometimes this looks like fight. You feel sharp. You snap. You argue. You become defensive. Everything feels like a threat.

Sometimes it looks like flight. You want to escape. You withdraw. You go busy. You avoid the conversation. You disappear emotionally, or literally leave the room.

Sometimes it looks like freeze. You go blank. You can't think. You can't speak. You feel stuck. You might look calm from the outside while your system is flooded inside.

Sometimes it looks like fawn. You become hyper-agreeable. You over-apologize. You try to keep the peace at all costs. You abandon your own needs in order to reduce risk.

In all of these, the core feature is the same: The CEO has lost access.

Not permanently. Not forever. But in that moment, your survival system has taken priority, and your ability to reason and choose is reduced.

This is Red.

And here is the most important thing to understand about Red: Red does not respond to analysis.

Red responds to stabilization. It responds to cues of safety that the nervous system can actually receive: rhythm, breath, sensation, movement, grounding, connection, containment.

That's what we're going to focus on in the rest of the chapter. But before we do, I want to offer one more idea that makes this even easier.

You don't have to identify your state perfectly.

You only need to know whether you are still in the zone where you can choose, or whether you've tipped into the zone where you need to stabilize first.

A simple question can help: "Can I access choice right now?"

If the answer is yes, even a little, you're likely in Yellow. Support yourself early. Shift state gently. You can change the trajectory.

If the answer is no, you're likely in Red. Stop trying to think your way out. Stabilize first. Help the body come down. The thinking will return.

And here's a helpful shortcut. If you can pause long enough to ask yourself that question, you're often not fully in Red yet. That means a small shift right now can change the whole trajectory.

This is the skill. Not perfection. Not constant calm. Just the ability to recognize what's happening and meet it with the right kind of support. And once you can do that, you stop fearing activation. You stop making it mean something about who you are.

You start treating it like weather. Something that moves through. Something you can work with. It's a process you can guide. That's where calm becomes real.

Part 3: What Actually Helps, in the Moment

Once you can recognize your state, the next question becomes much simpler: "What kind of support will actually land right now?"

This matters because when you're activated, it's very easy to reach for the wrong kind of help. It's easy to start explaining, or analyzing, or mentally negotiating with yourself.

But when your nervous system is in protection mode, it is not primarily listening to language. It is listening to physiology, rhythm, breath, muscle tension. It is listening to what your eyes are doing, how fast you're moving, and whether your body feels contained or exposed.

This is why the most effective real-time regulation is usually bottom-up. You start with the body, and the mind follows. When the body begins to settle, even slightly, access to thinking returns. The CEO comes back online.

The aim of real-time regulation is not to feel wonderful. It's to create enough shift that you can regain choice. Sometimes that means bringing yourself down from Red to Yellow. Sometimes it means stopping Yellow from tipping into Red. Sometimes it simply means staying present long enough to get through the moment without making it worse.

That's the win.

There are two different situations we need to talk about because what helps in Yellow is not the same as what helps in Red.

When You're in Yellow

Yellow is the state where you still have some access to choice. You might feel tense or urgent. You might feel irritated or anxious. You might feel like you're speeding up internally. But there is still a part of you watching it happen.

In Yellow, small shifts have a disproportionate impact. This is where regulation works best, because you're not trying to recover from a full hijack. You're changing the trajectory.

The simplest place to begin is the breath because breathing gives your nervous system direct information. A short, shallow breath tells your body, "We're under threat." A slower breath with a longer exhale tells your body, "We can stand down a notch." The exhale is especially powerful because it is associated with settling pathways in the nervous system. When you lengthen the exhale, even a little, you are changing the signal.

You don't need a perfect technique. You're not performing breathwork. You're simply giving your body a different rhythm for long enough that it can take the hint.

Yellow also responds well to what I call "softening the brace." Most people don't realize how much they are bracing until they stop. You can often shift state simply by undoing one piece of bracing and letting your body feel the difference. It might be your jaw, or your shoulders, or your hands. One small release can create a cascade, because the nervous system reads muscle tension as part of its threat calculation.

You can also work with attention. Activation narrows attention. It locks onto the problem. In Yellow, you can deliberately widen attention without needing to do anything dramatic. You can let your eyes move around the space you're in. You can orient to what is here, now, rather than what your mind is predicting. This is not positive thinking. It's a physiological cue that tells the nervous system, "We are not trapped."

Yellow is often just a system that needs a small downshift. And if you do it early enough, you change the whole moment.

When You're in Red

Red is different.

In Red, you're no longer aiming for insight. You're aiming for stabilization.

This is the state where people often panic about their own experience. They start thinking, "I shouldn't be like this," or "I need to calm down now," which unfortunately adds another layer of threat to the threat response.

So the first step in Red is not a technique. The first step is permission.

This is a nervous system event. It will pass. The job is to help your body get through it.

In Red, words tend to inflame rather than soothe. Explaining, arguing, defending yourself, trying to find the perfect sentence, or trying to think your way out can all increase activation because they require cognitive resources you don't have access to right now.

Red-state moments don't just feel intense. They can feel destabilizing because they threaten identity. You think, "I'm not this kind of person," or "If I lose control here, what does that say about me?" That fear adds a second layer of activation. Now your nervous system isn't only responding to the original trigger. It is also defending against shame.

This is why these moments can spiral. And it's why they deserve support, not judgment. In Red, success is not the perfect response. Success is getting through the moment without escalating further, creating safety afterward, and coming back to yourself sooner than you used to.

So in Red, the most helpful move is often to reduce complexity.

Fewer words. Fewer decisions. Less input.

If you can pause speech, do. If you can step away from the conversation briefly, do. If you can stop engaging with the thing that is escalating you, do. This is not avoidance. This is containment. It is giving your nervous system a chance to come down.

Red responds well to the most basic signals of safety: a slower rhythm, a grounded body, and a sense of physical containment.

Sometimes that containment is as simple as feeling your feet on the floor and pressing them gently down. Sometimes it's placing a hand on your chest or your abdomen, not as a dramatic gesture, but as a cue of support. Sometimes it's sitting back in a chair and letting the chair hold you, instead of holding yourself up with tension. Sometimes it's moving to a quieter space, or turning down stimulus, because in high activation, the nervous system becomes more sensitive to noise, light, and interruption.

Red also often needs completion. If your body has mobilized energy (fight or flight energy), it may need a safe way to discharge it. That doesn't have to be a workout. It can be as small as shaking out your hands, rolling your shoulders, standing and pressing your palms firmly against a wall, or taking a short walk to let your body feel movement and resolution. These aren't random tricks. They are ways of telling your nervous system, "The energy has somewhere to go."

One of the fastest ways to shift Red is through temperature because temperature is a direct physiological signal. Cool water on the face, holding something cold, or stepping into fresh air can interrupt the spiral because they change what the body is perceiving. Your nervous system pays attention to temperature as part of its safety detection system.

And then there's connection. Not "talk it out." Not "explain yourself better." But co-regulation.

Sometimes the most regulating thing is simply being with someone who is steady. A calm tone. A grounded presence. A person who isn't trying to fix you but helps your body feel, "I'm not alone, and I'm not in trouble." If you have access to that kind of support, it can be profoundly settling because nervous systems borrow cues from each other.

The thread that runs through all of this is simple.

In Red, your job is to reduce threat signals and increase safety signals just long enough for the wave to peak and pass.

You're not trying to win the argument, solve the problem, or become a perfect person in the middle of a nervous system surge.

You're trying to come back into a state where choice is possible again.

And it will be. Because states move. They rise, they peak, and they fall.

The skill is learning how to help them fall sooner, with less damage, and with less shame.

Part 4: A Simple Way to Respond When You're Activated

When people first learn regulation tools, they often imagine they need to remember a sequence. They picture themselves in a stressful moment, calmly recalling a perfect process, as if they're flipping through a manual in their head.

Real life does not work like that. In real life, the moment arrives fast. Your body reacts before your mind catches up. So the goal of this part is not to give you more things to remember. It's to give you a simple way to respond that works even when you are not at your best. The easiest way to do that is to make the response feel obvious.

When you're activated, there are only two questions that matter.

The first is: "Where am I right now?"

Not in a philosophical sense. In a nervous system sense. Am I still in the zone where choice is possible, or have I tipped into the zone where I need stabilization first?

The second is: "What would help my body stand down a notch?"

Not "What would make me feel amazing?" Not "What would fix the whole situation?" Just "What would bring the intensity down one step?"

If you can answer those two questions, you are already doing the work.

This way of responding becomes easier with practice.

This way of responding becomes easier with practice because your nervous system becomes more familiar with the pathway back. It learns, through repetition, that activation is not a dead end. It is a state you can move through.

There is another key idea here that people often miss. In real-time regulation, you are rarely trying to do one big thing. You are usually trying to do one small thing at the right time. And the right time is earlier than you think.

Most people wait until they are overwhelmed to use their tools, and then they decide the tools don't work. But tools used at the first sign of activation work differently. They don't have to fight a full nervous system surge. They simply interrupt the climb.

This is why noticing matters.

Noticing is not a passive skill. Noticing is the moment you get to choose. And at first, you will notice late. That's normal. You will notice after you've snapped, after you've spiraled, after you've shut down. That does not mean you're failing. It means you're learning. Your awareness is catching up.

Then, slowly, you start noticing a little earlier. You notice the jaw tension before the sharp words; the racing thoughts before the spiral; the urge to escape before you disappear; the tightening before the flood.

That earlier noticing is baseline change in motion. It's the nervous system learning that it doesn't have to wait until the alarm is blaring before it gets support.

And this is what I want to make crystal clear: Real-time regulation is not about controlling yourself. It is about supporting yourself. It is about becoming the kind of person your nervous system trusts because you respond to activation with care rather than criticism. That trust is what makes calm more accessible, even in the middle of real life.

You don't need a long list of tools for this to work. In fact, the more activated you are, the less you'll remember. Pick two defaults now: one for Yellow and one for Red. A Yellow default might be a longer exhale and softening the brace. A Red default might be reducing input and grounding through your body. Familiarity beats variety. Your nervous system learns the way back through repetition.

Closing: Calm Is the Ability to Return

When you're activated, it isn't that you've suddenly become a worse version of yourself. It's that your nervous system has shifted into protection mode. That shift changes your breath, your body, your attention, and how easily you can access words, perspective, patience, and choice.

This is why trying to think your way out of high activation can feel impossible. Remember: State comes before story.

In real time, your first job is not insight. Your first job is support. You help the body stand down a notch, and the mind comes back online. The CEO returns. Choice becomes possible again.

Sometimes, regulation looks like a small pause and a longer exhale in a meeting. Sometimes it looks like not pressing send when the surge hits. Sometimes it looks like softening your face and slowing your voice when someone else is melting down. Sometimes it looks like stepping away for a moment because you can feel yourself tipping over.

None of this is about being perfect. It's about learning to meet your nervous system where it is.

And the deeper shift is this: The more often you respond to activation with care instead of criticism, the more your nervous system begins to trust you. It learns that it doesn't have to escalate in order to be noticed. It learns that stress does not have to become a crisis before it gets support.

That trust changes everything. Because calm is not the absence of activation. Calm is the ability to return.

Every time you practice returning, even imperfectly, you're training the system that runs your life.

CHAPTER 7

WHEN CALM BECOMES A BASELINE

Why the Same Tools Work Better on Some Days Than Others

By the end of Chapter 6, something important became clear.

When you're activated, it isn't a moral failing. It isn't immaturity. It isn't "not trying hard enough." It's a state.

And once you understand state, you stop taking your reactions so personally. You stop making them mean something about your worth. You start meeting them with support instead of shame.

That alone changes a nervous system.

But there's another moment that often comes right after that learning, a moment people don't always expect.

They start using the tools. They start noticing earlier. They start recovering more quickly. And yet they still have days where it all feels . . . harder than it should.

The same breath that helped yesterday barely touches the sides today. The same grounding that worked last week doesn't land. The same "I can handle this" mindset feels like it's spoken in a foreign language.

If that's your experience, I want you to hear this first: Nothing has gone wrong.

This isn't you "backsliding." It isn't proof that you're not improving. It isn't evidence that the tools don't work. It's simply a sign that you're ready for the next layer.

Because regulating in real time is one kind of skill. But making calm more available in your everyday life is another.

And that's what this chapter is about. Not how to fix yourself. Not how to become a permanently serene person who never gets rattled. It's about understanding why calm can feel close one day and far away the next, why some moments hit harder than others, and what changes when calm stops being a rescue mission and starts becoming a baseline.

PART 1: WHY CALM DOESN'T "STICK" YET

There's an assumption many people carry without realizing it: "If I know how to regulate, I should feel calm more often."

It makes sense. It's logical. It's what we all hope is true.

But nervous systems aren't primarily logical. They're protective.

And regulation is not the same thing as having a calm baseline.

Regulation is what you do when activation is already happening. It's the support you bring to a system that has already started mobilizing. It's how you guide yourself back toward steadiness when you've tipped into stress.

Baseline is different.

Baseline is what your body is running in the background before anything even happens. It's the "starting point" you live from.

That starting point matters more than most people realize.

Because a day that starts from a lower baseline gives you more room. You have more capacity. You have more tolerance. You can absorb a little stress without spilling over. You can handle a disruption without feeling as if it's the final straw.

A day that starts from a higher baseline is like starting the day already carrying a heavy bag. Nothing dramatic has happened yet, but you're already loaded. You're already closer to the edge. So small things hit bigger, and normal demands feel unreasonable.

This is why two days can look similar on paper and feel completely different in your body.

On one day, a last-minute change feels annoying but manageable. You sigh, you adjust, you move on.

On another day, the same kind of change feels like a personal attack from the universe. You can feel the heat in your chest. Your jaw tightens. Your thoughts speed up. You're suddenly ten seconds away from snapping at someone who doesn't deserve it.

And then the shame tries to show up. "What is wrong with me?" "Why can't I just handle things like other people?" "I thought I was doing better."

But it isn't a character flaw. It's capacity.

It's the difference between a system that has room and a system that is already full.

Which means the question isn't only "Can I regulate when I'm activated?" The bigger question becomes "How activated am I, starting out?"

That's baseline work. And it's where calm begins to feel less random.

PART 2: BASELINE – YOUR NERVOUS SYSTEM'S HOME SETTING

Baseline is the level of activation your nervous system returns to when life is ordinary. Not life on holiday. Not life in a meditation retreat. Just . . . normal life.

It's how your body feels when nothing is going wrong, but nothing is actively soothing you either.

For some people, "normal" includes a quiet steadiness. There's a sense of space in the body. There's a little buffer. Stress still happens, but the system recovers.

For others, "normal" includes tension even when the day is fine. The shoulders sit high without permission. The jaw tightens in meetings. The breath stays shallow. The mind runs ahead. Rest feels oddly uncomfortable, like something you should earn.

A high baseline can look like productivity on the outside and bracing on the inside.

And here's the tricky part: A high baseline often disguises itself as personality.

People say things like, "I'm just an anxious person." Or, "I'm just intense." Or, "I've always been like this." Or, "I'm not the kind of person who can relax."

Sometimes that's true. Temperament is real.

But very often, what people call personality is actually physiology. It's a nervous system that has learned, through experience, that it needs to stay ready. Ready for the next problem. Ready for the next demand. Ready for the next thing that might go wrong.

Even if your life is safe in the external sense, your body may still be living with the internal expectation of pressure, unpredictability, or threat. And when a body expects threat, it doesn't relax just because you ask it to. It relaxes when it has evidence.

Evidence that there is enough support. Evidence that stress doesn't last forever. Evidence that recovery is allowed. Evidence that you can feel something without getting overwhelmed.

That's why baseline change is not about forcing calm. It's about teaching your nervous system, slowly and consistently, that it can stand down more often.

This is the point where many people feel an unexpected wave of relief. Because it reframes everything.

If calm feels unavailable, it doesn't mean you're failing. It may simply mean your baseline is high.

And if your baseline is high, it makes perfect sense that you need more support than someone whose system starts the day with more room.

That's not weakness. That's information. And information is something we can work with.

PART 3: WHAT SHAPES BASELINE

Once you start noticing baseline, you can't unsee it. You'll begin to recognize the days when your body feels like it has room. You'll also recognize the days where you wake up already braced, already running, already slightly irritated by the fact that another day is happening.

And it becomes obvious that baseline isn't random. It's responsive.

Your nervous system is not flipping coins in the morning to decide whether you're going to feel steady or brittle. It is taking in information and making a prediction about what kind of day it needs to prepare for.

That prediction is shaped by a few very human forces.

One of them is load.

Load is what your system is carrying, both on the surface and underneath. It includes the obvious things such as deadlines, conflict, responsibilities, and pressure. But it also includes the invisible things that don't look dramatic from the outside and still cost a lot internally: uncertainty, carrying too many decisions, feeling like you have to be the one who holds it together. It includes all the small moments where you override what your body is asking for because you have no choice or because you've trained yourself to keep going.

When load is high, your nervous system becomes more sensitive. There is less spare capacity. There is less buffer. There is less tolerance for "just one more thing."

That's why the same small inconvenience can feel like a mild annoyance one day and like the final straw another day. The inconvenience didn't change. Your available capacity did.

Another force is recovery.

Recovery is not a reward you earn when you finally finish everything. Recovery is how a nervous system returns to steadiness after it has mobilized. It is what allows the body to come down instead of staying quietly activated in the background.

When something stressful happens, your nervous system does not just "think a thought." It makes a physiological shift. The sympathetic branch of the nervous system increases arousal. Stress hormones such as adrenaline and cortisol are released to mobilize energy. Your body becomes more ready. Your attention narrows. Your muscles prepare. This is not drama. It is an ancient survival feature doing exactly what it was designed to do.

The problem is not the stress response. The problem is what happens after.

In the modern world, many of us activate and activate and activate, but we don't complete. The email is answered, but the body doesn't get the message. The conversation ends, but the nervous system stays alert. The meeting finishes, but the system doesn't fully stand down. We move straight into the next demand, and the activation that was meant to be temporary becomes the background setting.

That lingering is what people often call being "on edge for no reason." It isn't for no reason. It's residue.

There's a story that captures this beautifully. When a gazelle runs from a lion and escapes, it doesn't stand there and mentally process what happened. It often shakes. Its body tremors. The gazelle is not weak or being dramatic, and it is no longer in danger, but its nervous system is discharging the energy of survival. The danger has passed, but the activation is still in the body, and the body completes the cycle through movement.

Humans are built with the same basic machinery.

We might not shake dramatically after a tense phone call, but the physiology underneath is similar. When stress mobilizes energy and there is no completion, the body can stay partially "on." That can show up as restlessness, tightness, irritability, a racing mind, or that wired-but-tired feeling where you're exhausted and still can't properly settle.

This is why recovery that truly allows your system to downshift matters so much. It is not indulgence or laziness. It is not something you have to earn. It is biology finishing what it started.

The third force is something most people don't talk about because it sounds too simple until you feel it: safety signals.

People assume safety is a fact. Either you are safe, or you are not. But safety, to the nervous system, is a felt experience. It is something the body decides based on cues. Your thinking brain can know you're fine, but your nervous system is asking a different question: "Do I have evidence, right now, that I can stand down?"

Your body reads your breath. It reads your muscle tension. It reads the pace of your movements. It reads whether you are rushing, bracing, scanning, preparing. It reads the tone of voices around you. It reads whether there is warmth, predictability, connection, or spaciousness.

When those cues are present, the parasympathetic system, including pathways of the vagus nerve, can help bring the body back toward regulation. When those cues are scarce, your system stays in a low-level "ready" state, even if nothing is actively threatening you.

This is why you can be objectively safe and still not feel safe. It's also why you can be in the middle of a hard day and still find moments of steadiness. It isn't because the day became easy. It's because your nervous system received a signal that it could stand down, even briefly.

When baseline is high, it often means one of three things is happening: Either the load is high, or recovery is low, or safety signals are scarce. Sometimes all three are true at once, which is why some seasons of life can feel like living with your nervous system permanently half-raised, always ready, always slightly tense.

This is not bad news. It is not a diagnosis of "you will always be like this." It's the opposite.

If baseline is shaped by these forces, baseline can be changed by working with these forces. Not by forcing yourself to calm down, mentally lecturing your body, or trying to build a perfectly regulated life, but by changing the kind of evidence your nervous system receives over time.

And that brings us to the next question.

If baseline is shaped by load, recovery, and safety signals, what does it look like to influence those things in a real life that is still busy, still imperfect, still full of demands?

That is where calm becomes practical.

Part 4: How Calm Becomes Practical in Real Life

Once you understand baseline, a lot of your "why am I like this?" questions start to soften. You stop treating activation as a surprise attack. You start seeing it as information. You can often trace it back to something very ordinary: too much load, not enough recovery, not enough safety.

The next question is the one that actually matters: If baseline is shaped by these forces, what do you do with that knowledge in a life that is still busy, still imperfect, still full?

This is where many people accidentally make it harder than it needs to be. They hear "baseline change" and imagine they need a new lifestyle. They picture morning routines that require a spreadsheet, a meditation cushion, and a strong relationship with dawn. They assume the only path to calm is a complete restructure of life, and if they can't do that, they do nothing.

But baseline does not change because you do one impressive thing occasionally. Baseline changes because your nervous system receives different evidence repeatedly.

That word is worth sitting with for a moment: evidence.

Your nervous system does not respond to your intention. It responds to what it experiences. It responds to what happens in your body again and again until it becomes believable.

This is why the most powerful baseline work is often quiet. It happens inside ordinary moments. It happens in ways that don't look like "self-care" at all. It often takes less time than you think, and it often feels almost too small to matter.

And yet it matters, because it interrupts the pattern that keeps baseline high.

Most people don't spend their days in one continuous state of panic or overwhelm. They spend their days in a series of small activations. A tense email. A rushed transition. A difficult conversation. A moment of overstimulation. A spike of worry. A tight deadline. A child melting down. A colleague's tone. A thought that spirals.

On their own, these moments are manageable. The issue is what happens when they stack without completion.

The body mobilizes, but never fully discharges. The system is aroused, but never quite returns. You keep moving, because you have to, and because you're capable, and because there is always another thing. By the end of the day, your nervous system is still carrying a collection of unfinished stress responses, and your baseline is quietly elevated, even if nothing is currently "wrong."

This is why the idea of micro-recovery is so important, but I want to be careful with how I say that, because it can easily sound like one more thing you should be doing. It isn't. This is not about adding tasks to your day. It's about building tiny moments of completion to the tasks you already have, so your nervous system doesn't have to hold everything until later.

Think back to the gazelle. It doesn't schedule an hour of shaking at 6 p.m. It doesn't wait until the weekend. It completes the stress response as soon as it can because completion is what resets the system.

Humans are capable of the same kind of completion, but we often miss the moment when it's available. We move straight from stress into the next demand. We override our bodies. We tell ourselves we'll calm down later. And then later arrives, and we're too depleted to do anything except scroll, snack, or collapse.

Baseline work becomes practical when you start noticing the small windows where completion is possible.

A transition is one of those windows. You stand up from your desk. You leave a meeting. You get out of the car. You finish a phone call. You walk from one room into another. You move from work mode into home mode. You step away from a difficult conversation, and there's a pause before the next thing.

Those are moments when the nervous system can either carry stress forward or discharge it.

When you take even a brief moment to signal completion, you lower the amount of stress your nervous system has to hold.

That signal might be a slow exhale. It might be relaxing your shoulders. It might be letting your jaw unclench. It might be feeling your feet on the ground before you walk into the next environment. It might be a gentle shake of the hands after a tense conversation.

It might be moving your body in a way that tells the system, "It's done."

From the outside, it looks like nothing. Inside, your nervous system receives a message that it rarely gets in modern life: We mobilized, we survived, we completed, we can come down now.

When those messages happen often enough, your baseline changes because your body learns that activation does not have to last all day.

There is another practical truth here, and it can be surprisingly freeing: Calm is often created by subtraction.

Many people assume the solution is to "do more" in order to feel better. But for nervous systems that are already overloaded, doing more can become another form of pressure.

Sometimes, the most regulating thing you can do is remove one layer. Not remove it forever. Not remove it perfectly. Just reduce the load enough that your system stops bracing.

This might look like slowing the first movement of the day instead of launching straight into urgency. It might look like turning down a background noise you've learned to tolerate. It might look like closing one open loop or making one decision in advance, so you don't have to carry it mentally. It might look like having fewer inputs at the end of the day, so your body can stand down.

It might look like saying no to one thing, because although you could do it, you want your nervous system to have evidence that you don't always override yourself.

That is the deeper point. Baseline change happens when your nervous system experiences you as someone who pays attention. Someone who notices when it is activated. Someone who helps it complete. Someone who makes room for recovery. Someone who creates safety signals, not through perfection, but through consistency.

And that's why this chapter is not a lifestyle overhaul. It's a shift in relationship.

You are building a pattern where activation is not the enemy, and calm is not a heroic achievement. Calm becomes something your nervous system can access more often because you are giving it a life that is slightly more complete, slightly more supported, and slightly less full.

Part 5: The Choices That Quietly Raise Baseline And the Ones That Lower It

Once you start seeing baseline, you also start seeing why it rises. Baseline rises because your nervous system is doing its job. It's taking in information, scanning for what's coming, and preparing you for what might be required.

That means baseline is influenced, every day, by conditions and choices that often have nothing to do with willpower. Many of them feel normal. Many are culturally rewarded. Some even look like success.

And yet your nervous system experiences them as demand.

One of the most common baseline-raisers is constant urgency.

Urgency isn't just a busy day. Urgency has a particular feel in the body. It's the way you walk faster than you need to. It's the way you start doing the next thing before you've finished the current thing. It's the tightness in the chest as you check the time for the third time in two minutes. It's the subtle belief that you're behind before you've even started.

When urgency becomes your default pace, your nervous system takes it literally. Faster pace and rushed movement are not neutral signals to the body. They are cues that something matters, something is at stake, something might go wrong if you slow down. If your day is lived in a constant state of "hurry," your body never gets enough evidence that it can stand down.

Another baseline-raiser is unfinished business.

This isn't only the big unfinished business. It's also the small open loops that hum quietly in the background of your mind. The email you saw and didn't respond to. The appointment you need to book. The permission slip you forgot. The message you keep meaning to send. The half-done task you left mid-stream because someone needed you.

Your brain is designed to hold onto incomplete things. It's one of the ways it tries to protect you from forgetting something important. But there's a cost to being mentally "on call" all day. Even when you're doing something else, part of your attention remains slightly activated because it knows there are loose ends. Those loose ends become load.

This is why closing a small loop can create an immediate sense of relief that feels bigger than the task itself. The relief isn't you being dramatic. It's your nervous system registering completion.

Decision fatigue is another baseline-raiser, and it's one of the most underestimated.

Most people imagine decision fatigue as something that happens after major decisions, like changing jobs or moving house. But the nervous system is not only mobilized by big decisions. It's mobilized by constant decisions.

Every time you decide, you use executive function. Executive function is the brain's ability to plan, choose, inhibit impulses, and hold multiple options in mind. It relies heavily on the prefrontal cortex, and it is very sensitive to stress, sleep loss, and cognitive overload. In simple terms, the part of your brain that makes good choices is the same part that gets tired when life is demanding.

This is why deciding what to have for dinner can feel absurdly hard, even when you're a competent adult who makes far more important decisions at work.

By the time dinner arrives, your brain has often spent a whole day prioritizing, responding, switching tasks, and managing people. Your nervous system has handled constant micro-demands and tiny self-control moments. The prefrontal cortex is tired, and your system wants relief, not another round of "evaluate options."

So you open the fridge and stare at it as if it might offer emotional support.

You might notice yourself thinking, "I don't care. I just can't decide." Or you feel oddly irritated by the question itself. Dinner isn't a big deal, but your decision-making capacity has been used up on a hundred small choices you didn't even notice you were making.

This is why meal planning can feel like a life upgrade even when it's not glamorous.

Meal planning doesn't just save time. It removes a repeated decision at the end of the day when your capacity is low. It takes a recurring point of friction and turns it into a known outcome. Your nervous system experiences that as a reduction in load and a small increase in predictability. Both of those lower baseline.

This same logic is why some tech entrepreneurs famously wore the same outfit every day. The black t-shirt wasn't a fashion statement. It was decision conservation.

If you remove the daily question of "What should I wear?", you remove a small drain. One less decision. One less moment of evaluation. One less opportunity for your nervous system to mobilize.

It's not that a black t-shirt makes you calmer. It's that fewer decisions make you less loaded. And when you're less loaded, you're less reactive.

Another baseline-raiser is sensory pressure.

We tend to underestimate sensory load because it doesn't always register as "stress" in the way we expect. But your nervous system doesn't only respond to emotional events. It responds to the environment.

Bright lights, constant background noise, crowded spaces, multiple conversations, the hum of notifications, the pressure of being "reachable," the constant switching between screens, the low-level sound of the news, the ever-present ping of "one more thing."

None of these is inherently dangerous, but they are activating. They demand attention, even when you think you're ignoring them. They keep the system oriented outward, scanning, responding, taking in more than it can easily process.

The brain also treats interruption as a kind of threat in miniature. Every time your focus is pulled away, your system has to reorient. Your attention narrows, widens, narrows again. This constant switching costs energy. It increases cognitive load. And it can keep your baseline slightly elevated throughout the day without you ever feeling a single dramatic spike.

This is one of the reasons people feel calmer when they are somewhere quiet, even if nothing else changes. It isn't mystical. It's nervous system math.

Another baseline-raiser is disconnection.

Not just loneliness but the subtler kind: being around people while feeling like you have to hold yourself together alone. Feeling like you can't soften. Feeling like you can't be honest. Feeling like you have to manage the room.

Humans are built for co-regulation. Our nervous systems settle through safe connection. Tone of voice, facial expression, presence, and predictability all matter. When connection feels unsafe, or when you feel like you have to perform or brace, your system doesn't receive the cues it needs to stand down.

That doesn't mean you need constant socializing to feel regulated. It means you need some reliable experience of safety, whether that comes through relationships, routines, or environments that your body reads as steady.

And then there's chronic override.

This is the baseline-raiser that often hides in plain sight because it looks like competence.

Override is when your body signals something, and you push past it. You ignore hunger because you're busy. You ignore fatigue because there's more to do. You ignore the need for a pause because you don't want to "waste time." You ignore stress signals because you've trained yourself to function through them.

Sometimes override is unavoidable. Life doesn't always offer gentle pacing. Many people are carrying responsibilities that make "listen to your body" sound like a luxury.

But when override becomes a long-term pattern, the nervous system adapts. It learns that you are not available as support. It learns that it must stay ready, because rest is not reliable and needs are not consistently met.

That learning raises baseline.

It makes calm harder to access because the nervous system doesn't expect it.

If you look at these baseline-raisers closely, you'll notice a theme. None of them is a personal flaw. They are signals. They are information your nervous system uses to decide whether it needs to stay mobilized or whether it can afford to stand down.

Which is why the baseline-lowerers are not complicated. They are simply the opposite signals.

A slower pace, even briefly, tells the body there isn't an emergency. Completion tells the body that the stress cycle can close. Fewer open loops tell the body there is less to carry. Fewer decisions tell the body it can stop evaluating. Less input tells the body it can stop scanning. A reliable moment of connection tells the body it does not have to do everything alone. A small act of support tells the body it can trust you again.

This is not about doing everything. It is about knowing what you're doing.

When you understand what raises baseline, you stop blaming yourself for struggling in a system that is overloaded. And when you understand what lowers baseline, you stop treating calm as a personality trait you either have or you don't.

You start creating calm on purpose, in ways that fit the life you actually live.

PART 6: THE CHOICES THAT QUIETLY LOWER BASELINE

If baseline rises when your system receives signals of demand, urgency, overload, and uncertainty, then it lowers when your system receives the opposite signals. It lowers when life becomes even slightly more complete, slightly more predictable, slightly less noisy, and slightly more supportive.

The first baseline-lowerer is **pace**.

This is not about living slowly. It's about giving your nervous system moments where it can feel that you are not in a chase. A slightly slower pace is one of the most powerful safety signals you can offer because the body reads speed as meaning. When you move quickly, your system assumes something is urgent. When you move with intention, even briefly, the system gets evidence that there is no immediate threat.

This is why the first minute of your morning matters more than people think. If you launch out of bed and immediately grab your phone, your body can interpret that as "we're behind already." If the first minute includes even a small pause, a slower movement, or one breath that is not rushed, you have quietly told your nervous system, "We're not starting the day in emergency mode."

It's also why a calm, unhurried first movement after work can change an entire evening. If you walk into the house like you're sprinting from the day, your system brings that urgency with you. If you arrive at a slightly slower pace, you give yourself a better starting point.

The second baseline-lowerer is **completion**.

Completion is the opposite of carrying residue. It's the message your body gets when it understands "That's over." This is why a short walk after a stressful day can feel surprisingly effective. Walking isn't magical, but movement is one of the simplest ways for the body to discharge stress activation and return toward regulation.

Completion can also be much smaller than people imagine. It can be the exhale you allow after you press send on a difficult email. It can be the moment you notice your shoulders are up around your ears and you let them drop. It can be the quiet physical unwinding that happens when you step away from tension and allow your body to come down rather than forcing yourself to stay "on."

When completion happens often enough, the nervous system begins to trust that activation does not last forever. That trust lowers baseline.

The third baseline-lowerer is **closing loops**.

This is where the psychology of relief meets the biology of load. A small unfinished task can take up more nervous system space than it deserves because your brain keeps it slightly "active" to protect you from forgetting it. When you close the loop, your attention softens. You can feel the internal unclenching.

This is why people often feel calmer after they finally book the appointment, reply to the message, or make the decision they've been postponing. It is rarely the task itself that brings relief. It is the removal of the mental holding pattern.

You can see this clearly in the way people avoid their inbox when they feel overloaded. The avoidance isn't laziness. It's a protective response. Your system knows it cannot handle more open loops, so it tries to avoid the place where open loops multiply. Closing loops, gently and strategically, reduces that background pressure and lowers baseline.

The fourth baseline-lowerer is **predictability**.

Predictability is not about boring routines. It's about nervous system stability. When your body knows what's coming next, even in a small way, it reduces scanning. It reduces vigilance. It allows the system to stand down because it doesn't have to keep guessing.

This is why meal planning helps even when you don't love meal planning. It removes the daily "what's for dinner?" decision at the exact time when your decision-making capacity is lowest. It's why having a default breakfast or a short list of "house meals" can feel calming. It's why packing a bag the night before can reduce morning stress disproportionally.

The brain relaxes when it doesn't have to solve the same problem repeatedly under pressure.

The fifth baseline-lowerer is **reducing input**.

Most nervous systems are not designed for constant high-volume information. When you reduce input, you reduce scanning. You reduce interruption. You reduce the ongoing demand placed on attention.

Reducing input can be as simple as turning off a nonessential notification stream. It can be putting your phone in another room while you do one task. It can be creating pockets of quiet where your nervous system doesn't have to track multiple sources of stimulation.

This is why people often feel more regulated in nature, even if they are still thinking about their problems. Nature tends to reduce the sensory and cognitive demands that keep the nervous system on high alert. It widens attention instead of narrowing it. It gives the system evidence of spaciousness.

The sixth baseline-lowerer is **connection**.

This is not about being around people all the time. It's about safe co-regulation. A nervous system relaxes in the presence of steadiness. Humans are wired to take cues from each other's tone, facial expression, pace, and presence.

This is why a conversation with the right person can lower your baseline even if nothing is solved. Your body receives a signal: "I am not alone in this." That signal matters. It is not sentimental. It is physiological.

Connection can also come from being understood. Being seen. Being able to speak honestly without punishment. Which brings us to a concept that belongs here because it is, at its core, a nervous system phenomenon: psychological safety.

Psychological safety is not just something teams talk about. It's the felt sense that you can be human without danger. It's the experience of being able to ask a question, admit a mistake, say "I'm not okay," or share an idea without being shamed, ridiculed, dismissed, or punished.

When psychological safety is present, your nervous system spends less time bracing. You don't have to rehearse what you're going to say. You don't have to monitor yourself constantly. You don't have to scan for threat in the response. That reduces load, and it increases safety signals at the same time.

When psychological safety is absent, baseline rises. Even small interactions can feel risky. Your system becomes vigilant. It prepares for judgment. It tightens. It stays alert. You might still function well, but the cost is higher.

This matters in workplaces, of course, but it also matters at home. It matters in friendships. It matters in family dynamics. Any environment where you feel you have to perform or protect yourself will tend to raise baseline over time.

Finally, one of the most powerful baseline-lowerers is **self-support**.

This is not self-indulgence. It is the nervous system learning that you are available.

Self-support looks like eating before you crash; noticing you're at capacity and adjusting instead of overriding; taking a pause before you break. It looks like doing something small that helps your body stand down and trusting that this is not wasted time.

If chronic override raises baseline because the nervous system learns "My needs don't matter," then self-support lowers baseline because the nervous system learns the opposite.

It learns "Someone is paying attention." It learns "We can recover." It learns, "I don't have to do this alone." Even when you are the someone.

When you put these baseline-lowerers together, a pattern emerges. They are not complicated hacks. They are signals. They are the kind of evidence that tells a nervous system, again and again, that life is manageable and that activation can end.

And when the nervous system begins to believe that, calm stops being something you chase. It becomes something you return to.

Part 7: What Baseline Change Feels Like

Baseline change rarely announces itself with fireworks. Most people don't wake up one morning and think, "Ah, yes, today my nervous system is healed." If anything, baseline change is easy to miss because it happens in the spaces between the dramatic moments.

It shows up as a little more room. A small inconvenience still annoys you, but it doesn't hijack you. A conversation still feels uncomfortable, but you don't carry it for hours. A stressful day still happens, but you recover faster. You still have emotions, but your emotions don't feel like emergencies.

And perhaps most importantly, you stop being frightened of your own internal weather. You stop scanning yourself for signs you're about to "lose it." You stop living with that quiet dread that one more demand will send you over the edge. You start trusting that even if you spike, you can come back.

This is one of the most underestimated forms of freedom. Because when you don't trust your recovery, your whole life gets organized around prevention. You try to control everything so you don't tip over. You avoid situations that feel unpredictable. You become hyper-responsible. You become hyper-vigilant. You do the emotional equivalent of walking around with your shoulders up, braced for impact.

When baseline begins to lower, you don't just feel calmer. You feel safer inside yourself.

That safety doesn't mean your life becomes easy. It means your body becomes less convinced that life is a constant threat. You still meet challenges, but you meet them with more capacity. You still have pressure, but you're not permanently carrying it in your muscles and breath.

It also changes the way you interpret yourself. Instead of thinking, "Why am I like this?" you start thinking, "Ah. My system is loaded." Instead of spiraling into shame, you shift toward support. Instead of feeling trapped in your reactions, you become curious about your conditions.

That is a profound upgrade. And it's the kind of upgrade that compounds.

The more often your nervous system experiences completion, recovery, and safety signals, the more it expects them. The more it expects them, the less it stays on high alert. The less it stays on high alert, the easier it becomes to access the Calm Gap you learned about in Chapter 6.

This is why the work stacks. Regulation helps baseline. Baseline helps regulation. Each layer makes the next layer easier.

There is also something else that happens when baseline changes. You begin to notice that calm isn't only the absence of stress. Calm is presence.

It's the ability to be with your own life without bracing against it. It's being able to sit in a moment and actually feel it, instead of rushing past it internally. It's being able to respond to the people you love without feeling as if you're managing them. It's being able to experience a full day without your nervous system acting like it's been through a war.

Not every day. But more days. And that is the point.

Baseline change is not perfection. It is probability.

You are not trying to guarantee calm. You are trying to make calm more likely.

Closing: Your Nervous System Learns from Evidence

If there is one sentence that could summarize this chapter, it might be this: Your nervous system learns from evidence, not intention.

If your baseline has been high for a long time, it makes sense that calm doesn't always feel available. Your system has been doing what it was designed to do: preparing, scanning, bracing, mobilizing, coping.

That is not a failure. It is adaptation. And adaptation can change.

Baseline begins to lower when load reduces, when recovery becomes real, and when safety signals become more frequent. It begins to lower when stress responses are completed instead of carried. It begins to lower when the pace of life becomes slightly more humane. It begins to lower when you stop living in constant override and start becoming someone your nervous system can trust.

This isn't a dramatic transformation. It's a quiet one.

It looks like a body that can come down. It looks like a mind that doesn't have to sprint. It looks like more room between stimulus and response. It looks like a life that feels less like constant management and more like something you can actually inhabit.

In the next chapter, we'll talk about why certain moments hit so hard, even when you "know better." We'll explore the way your nervous system responds not only to what's happening now but to what it has learned before. And once you understand that, you'll stop blaming yourself for being triggered by "small" things.

To a nervous system, nothing is small if it signals danger. And when you learn to read those signals, you gain something even better than control. You gain choice.

CHAPTER 8

TRIGGERS

WHEN THE PRESENT WAKES UP THE PAST

Some reactions don't build. They detonate.

You can be having an ordinary day, in an ordinary conversation, and then a single moment lands with surprising force. A tone. A look. A pause. A comment that seems small on paper and massive in your body.

Your chest tightens. Your stomach drops. Heat rises. Your mind either races or goes blank. You feel an urge to defend yourself, fix it, disappear, or win. And the confusing part is that a moment ago, you were fine.

This is the experience that makes people question themselves. They tell themselves they're overreacting. They tell themselves they should be past this. They try to talk themselves out of it, and the talking only makes it louder.

So let's name what's happening, clearly.

Some stress responses are about what is happening now. Trigger responses are about what is happening now *and* what it resembles.

This is the nervous system's version of pattern recognition: fast, automatic, protective. Your body is not waiting for your mind to debate whether the situation is "actually that bad." It is responding to a cue that, somewhere in your history, got linked with danger.

Sometimes that history is dramatic and obvious. Sometimes it's subtle. Sometimes it's relational. Sometimes it's a thousand tiny moments that taught your nervous system a rule.

And once a rule is learned, the nervous system tends to keep applying it until it has strong evidence that the rule is no longer needed.

That is what this chapter is about. Not analyzing you, blaming your childhood for everything, or turning your emotions into a project. This chapter is about learning to read trigger responses as information rather than failure, learning to spot the pattern beneath the moment, and learning how to update those old rules so your present stops getting hijacked by the past.

Part 1: Why "Small Things" Can Feel So Big

Most people assume a trigger is an exaggerated reaction to something minor. But from the nervous system's perspective, a trigger is not "minor." A trigger is a cue.

And cues don't have to be dramatic to be powerful. They just have to be familiar.

Your nervous system is built to scan for safety and danger. It does this automatically, under the surface of conscious thought. It reads faces, tone, pace, proximity, unpredictability, inclusion, exclusion. It reads whether you're being respected or dismissed, whether connection feels stable or at risk.

And if a cue resembles something that was once linked with pain or threat, your body can respond as if the original situation is happening again.

You're not being irrational. Your nervous system would rather over-protect than under-protect. It's like a smoke alarm that goes off when the toast burns. It's annoying, but it's designed that way for a reason. It would rather be wrong than miss a real fire.

Trigger responses are the human version of that. A look that reminds you of judgment. A tone that reminds you of being controlled. A silence that reminds you of disconnection. A delay that reminds you of being forgotten.

On the surface, the current moment might be a two out of ten. But if it activates an old template, your body responds as if it's an eight.

This is why trigger responses feel disproportionate. It isn't that your response is "too big." It's that your nervous system is responding to a meaning. And meaning lives in the body.

You can often tell the difference between normal stress and a trigger response by the speed of it. Normal stress tends to rise. A trigger response tends to be instantaneous. One second, you're in the conversation. The next second, you're braced, defending, collapsing, or leaving internally. The story changes quickly, too. Your mind starts generating explanations, accusations, worst-case scenarios, rehearsals. It tries to make sense of the sensation by building a narrative around it.

That narrative can feel convincing in the moment because it's being powered by chemistry. And then later, once your body settles, the story often changes. You look back and think, "Why did that feel so intense?"

That question is a clue. Trigger responses aren't always attached to clear memories. Often they're attached to implicit learning: what your nervous system learned through repetition, atmosphere, and pattern. The lesson might not be a sentence you can recall. It might be something your body learned, like a reflex.

The lesson might sound like:
"If I make a mistake, I'm not safe."
"If I upset someone, I'll lose connection."
"If I need too much, I'll be rejected."
"If I relax, something will go wrong."
"If I don't perform, I won't belong."

Most people don't consciously believe these things. But the nervous system doesn't operate on beliefs. It operates on predictions. It predicts what will happen next, based on what has happened before.

The moment your nervous system detects a trigger, it makes a prediction and mobilizes you for protection.

And once you understand that, the aim changes. The aim is not to eliminate emotion. The aim is to recognize what's happening early, meet it with steadiness, and update the prediction over time. Because the present doesn't have to keep paying for an old lesson.

Part 2: Your Trigger Signature – The Pattern Beneath the Pattern

Once you understand that trigger responses are about resemblance, not logic, the next step becomes more practical. Instead of asking, "What's wrong with me?" you start asking, "What pattern is this?"

Because trigger responses aren't random. They have a signature. And when you can recognize your signature, you stop being blindsided. You stop treating intensity as failure. You start treating it as information.

Here's a helpful clue: If the reaction feels much bigger than the moment, it can be a sign you've bumped into something older than the present. Not always. Not as a hard rule. But often.

When the present moment is relatively small and your body responds as if it's enormous, that's not proof you're being dramatic. It's usually proof that your nervous system is responding to a familiar meaning—a meaning that was learned earlier, when you had fewer options, less power, and a stronger need to protect yourself quickly.

This is why trigger responses can feel confusing. Part of you can know you're safe. Part of you can know the person didn't mean it that way. Part of you can know you're not actually in danger. And yet your body reacts anyway.

That's because your nervous system doesn't wait for a full explanation. It responds to cues. It responds to tone, pace, expression, uncertainty, and the feeling of connection shifting. It responds to patterns it has seen before.

So instead of debating whether your reaction is "reasonable," we map it.

Various people can experience the same situation and have completely different trigger signatures.

One person goes into fight. They get sharp. They argue. They need to be right.

Another person goes into flight. They feel urgency. They want to leave, fix it, or escape the discomfort.

Another person goes into freeze. They go blank. They can't think. They can't speak.

Another person goes into fawn. They become agreeable, apologetic, eager to smooth it over.

These are not character flaws. They're protective strategies. They are the nervous system's attempt to solve a problem: stay safe, and stay connected.

A trigger signature is the pattern your system tends to run first. And mapping it doesn't make the trigger disappear overnight. But it does something just as important: It reduces the shame. When you can see the pattern, you stop making it mean something about who you are. You start seeing it as something your nervous system learned.

Here is a simple way to begin. The next time you notice a trigger response—or the next time you remember one clearly—walk through it like a curious observer.

Start with the body because the body tells the truth faster than the story.

What did your body do first? Maybe your chest tightened. Maybe your throat went dry. Maybe your stomach dropped. Maybe your face got hot. Maybe you felt restless energy in your hands or legs. Maybe you felt a sudden collapse, as if your system went offline.

Then notice what happened to your attention. Did it narrow onto the other person? Did you start scanning for danger in tone or expression? Did you start rehearsing what to say? Did you feel your mind searching for certainty? Did you disappear inward?

Then notice what happened to your impulse. Did you want to explain? Did you want to defend yourself? Did you want to fix it immediately? Did you want to leave? Did you want to shut down? Did you want to smooth it over, even if you weren't wrong?

Only then do you look at the meaning. Not the meaning your rational mind would choose. The meaning your nervous system assumed in that moment.

This is where the pattern beneath the pattern becomes visible. Because the surface trigger might change, but the underlying meaning often stays the same. Different day. Different person. Same internal conclusion.

> "I'm in trouble."
> "I'm not safe."
> "I'm about to be criticized."
> "I'm not important."
> "I'm going to lose connection."
> "I've done something wrong."

When you can name that meaning, you gain leverage. Not by forcing yourself to stop feeling it, but by responding to the right layer.

If the meaning is "I'm about to be rejected," your nervous system needs steadiness and safety cues before it can take in reassurance. If the meaning is "I'm in trouble," your nervous system needs containment before it can take in perspective. If the meaning is "I'm not safe," your nervous system needs signals of safety in the body before it can take in logic.

This is why mapping matters. It helps you stop trying to solve a nervous system problem with a thinking solution. And it also helps you see something else.

A trigger response is rarely just about the moment. It's often about a relationship theme: belonging, safety, worth, control, respect, abandonment, being seen, being too much.

When you see the theme, you stop feeling as though you're being taken out by random events. You start seeing the old rule your nervous system is trying to live by. And once you can see the rule, it becomes changeable.

Trigger responses are not proof that something is wrong with you. They are proof that your nervous system remembers what it learned. And the more compassion and clarity you bring to that remembering, the more freedom you create.

Part 3: How Triggers Actually Change – Repair, Re-patterning, and Updating the Old Rule

Once you can recognize a trigger response as a pattern, the natural next question is "How do I change it?"

This is where people often assume the answer has to be dramatic. They assume they need to dig up every memory. They assume they need to understand the trigger perfectly before it will soften. They assume they need to "heal it" in some big, final way.

Sometimes deeper work is needed, and we'll talk about that later. But most trigger change happens through something much quieter.

Trigger responses change when the nervous system has repeated experiences that contradict the old rule. Not once. Repeatedly.

Because the nervous system doesn't update from insight alone. It updates from evidence.

And evidence is not a sentence you tell yourself. Evidence is what your body lives through and survives. Evidence is what you experience with your nervous system still in your body.

If a trigger response reflects your system predicting danger, then change happens when your system learns "This situation is survivable." "I can stay connected and still be myself." "I can feel this and come back." "I can be imperfect and still belong." "I can be uncomfortable and still be safe."

That kind of learning doesn't happen in a single conversation with your mind. It happens through repair.

Repair is the missing skill no one teaches.

Most people think the problem is getting triggered. The bigger problem is what happens next. Because after a trigger, many people do one of two things: They escalate the situation and create fallout, or they retreat into shame and create isolation. Neither of those helps the nervous system update.

The nervous system updates through a third path: repair.

Repair is what you do after activation to restore safety, connection, and coherence. Sometimes, repair is between you and another person. Sometimes, repair is between you and yourself. Either way, repair sends a powerful message to your nervous system: "We can come back from this." And that message matters because it changes your baseline expectation.

If your nervous system has learned that conflict leads to disconnection, then repair is the evidence that conflict can be followed by reconnection. If your nervous system has learned that mistakes lead to punishment, then repair is the evidence that mistakes can be followed by kindness and learning. If your nervous system has learned that emotion leads to shame, then repair is the evidence that emotion can be held without humiliation.

Repair doesn't require a perfect apology or a long conversation. It requires one thing: restoring safety. That might look like naming what happened without blaming; taking space and then returning; softening your tone; making a small bid for connection. It might look like saying, simply, "I got activated. I'm back now." And sometimes repair is quieter than language. Sometimes repair is taking care of your body after a surge because your nervous system can't learn "this is safe now" if it's still flooded with adrenaline.

The activation response has a beginning, a middle, and an end.

One reason trigger responses keep repeating is that people treat them like emergencies that must be solved immediately. But a trigger is also a wave. It rises. It peaks. It falls. And that means you can work with it without forcing it.

The first goal is not to fix the story but to reduce activation. If you can bring the wave down even one notch, you create space for the CEO to return. And then something important becomes possible: You can choose what you do next.

This is where the real pattern change begins. Triggers become entrenched when the same ending happens every time: the same argument, the same withdrawal, the same over-apology, the same self-attack, the same silence, the same spiraling. The nervous system learns through repetition, and it repeats what it knows.

So when you want a trigger response to change, you don't start by trying to eliminate the beginning. You start by changing the ending. A slightly different ending is the beginning of a new pattern.

Re-patterning doesn't require big exposure.

People sometimes think they need to "face the trigger" at full intensity to heal it. But nervous systems don't update well when they are overwhelmed. Overwhelm teaches the system the same old lesson: "See? It was too much."

A more sustainable approach is to work within what you can tolerate. Small doses. Small wins. Small moments of "I stayed." Small moments of "I didn't abandon myself." Small moments of "I didn't escalate." Small moments of "I came back." This is how safety is built. Not by forcing yourself through the hardest version of the situation, but by showing your nervous system, repeatedly, that you can meet activation and return.

The Old Rule and the New Message

Most triggers contain an old rule. It's not always spoken, but it's there.

> "If I disappoint someone, I'm not safe."
> "If I speak up, I'll be punished."
> "If I relax, something will go wrong."
> "If I'm not perfect, I'll lose connection."
> "If I need too much, I'll be rejected."

You do not change this rule by arguing with it. You change it by sending a new message, at a level the nervous system can receive.

That message is usually very simple: "I'm here." "We're safe enough." "This is uncomfortable, not dangerous." "I can handle this." "I can come back."

Over time, the new message becomes more believable because it's paired with lived evidence. And slowly, the trigger loses its power because your nervous system stops treating it as an emergency.

What This Means in Real Life

In the moment of a trigger, you won't always be able to do the perfect thing, but you can practice the thing that changes patterns fastest: You can practice coming back.

That might mean pausing before you respond; stepping back and then returning; choosing a softer tone; naming your state instead of acting it out. It might mean doing a repair, even if it's small.

Every time you do that, you teach your nervous system something new. You teach it that activation is not a dead end, connection can be restored, and you don't have to become someone else to be safe.

And over time, those lessons accumulate. They become your new baseline, your new default.

This is how old trigger patterns change. Not in one breakthrough moment, but in the quiet accumulation of evidence that you can be here now, without being pulled back there.

Part 4: Trigger-Proofing the Next Moment – What to Do After a Trigger So It Has Less Power Next Time

There's a quiet myth that keeps people stuck: If you get triggered, you've failed. So the moment it happens, you either double down and push through, or you retreat into self-judgment and hope it doesn't happen again. Neither of those teaches the nervous system anything new.

What teaches the nervous system something new is what happens after the trigger. Because the trigger moment is often fast and automatic. But the minutes and hours that follow are where you can change the learning.

This part is about that window—not the perfect response in the heat of the moment but the reset that helps the next moment go differently.

Step One: Stabilize the Body First (the First Ten Minutes)

Right after a trigger, your nervous system is often still flooded. Even if the conversation is over, your body may still be braced for impact. Your thoughts might keep looping. Your stomach might still feel tight. Your heart might still be racing.

This is not the time to solve it. This is the time to come down.

The simplest question is "What would help my body stand down one notch?" Not ten notches. One.

It could be any of these: a longer exhale; unclenching your jaw; stepping outside for air; cool water on your face; shaking out your hands or rolling your shoulders; putting your feet on the ground and feeling the support underneath you.

You're not trying to perform calm. You're letting the chemistry move through because the nervous system can't learn a new lesson while it still believes the danger is present.

Step Two: Name What Happened Without Building a Case (Later That Day)

Once you've come down enough to think clearly again, this is the moment to do something small but powerful. You name the trigger without turning it into a courtroom drama.

> Not: "Here's why I'm right and they're wrong."
> Not: "Here's why I'm broken."
> Just: "Here's what happened in my system."

You're looking for three things: What was the cue? What was my signature? What meaning did my nervous system attach?

This can be a short mental review. It doesn't need journaling unless you like journaling.

For example: "The cue was that tone." "My signature was going sharp and defending." "The meaning was: I'm being judged / I'm in trouble."

This matters because it turns a confusing emotional storm into a recognizable pattern. And a pattern is workable.

Step Three: Add One New Ending (the Next Time It Happens)

This is the part most people miss. Triggers become entrenched because the ending is always the same: same escalation, same withdrawal, same apology, same shutdown, same shame spiral.

So when you want it to have less power next time, you don't aim to stop the trigger from appearing. You aim to create a slightly different ending.

A new ending could be tiny. It could be a pause before replying. It could be saying, "Give me a second." It could be lowering your voice rather than raising it. It could be stepping away and actually returning, instead of disappearing. It could be choosing one sentence that keeps you connected to yourself.

The nervous system learns from endings. If the old ending was "I was unsafe and alone," a new ending might be "I came back." If the old ending was "I had to please to stay safe," a new ending might be "I stayed kind without abandoning myself." If the old ending was "I exploded and then hated myself," a new ending might be "I noticed earlier and softened the brace."

Small changes count because small changes are repeatable. And repeatable is what rewires.

Step Four: Repair (If Another Person Was Involved)

Repair is not an admission of guilt. Repair is the act of restoring safety and connection after activation. Sometimes it's a conversation. Sometimes it's just a tone shift and a return.

The key is that repair happens from the CEO, not the Caveman. If you are still in Red, you wait. You're not avoiding the issue; you're choosing the state you want to bring to the conversation.

When you are ready, repair can be surprisingly simple. You can name your state without blaming: "I got activated earlier. I'm back now." You can own your behavior without self-attack: "I was sharper than I wanted to be." You can clarify what you need going forward: "Next time I'm feeling flooded, I'm going to take a minute before I respond." You can invite connection without forcing it: "I care about this, and I want us to be okay."

Even if the other person doesn't respond perfectly, doing repair teaches your nervous system something important: It is possible to come back.

Step Five: Don't Let Shame Become the Second Trigger

If you grew up learning that other people's emotions were your responsibility, boundaries will initially feel cruel. You may feel guilty just for having a limit, even if the limit is healthy and reasonable.

Guilt is not always a signal that you've done something wrong. Sometimes guilt is just a signal that you're doing something new.

You can let the guilt be there and still hold the line. Over time, your nervous system learns that guilt is survivable and that relationships can handle honesty.

That's how you move from "I have boundaries, but I feel terrible" to "I have boundaries, and I feel steady."

The Real Definition of Progress

Progress is not "I never get triggered." Progress is "I recognize it sooner." "I recover faster." "I do less damage." "I repair more quickly." "I don't abandon myself afterward." "I create a new ending."

That is how triggers lose power. Not by disappearing overnight but by becoming less convincing, less consuming, and less in charge. And when that happens, the present finally gets to be the present again.

PART 5: WHEN A TRIGGER IS AN OLD WOUND

By now, you've probably noticed something important. Some trigger responses soften surprisingly fast once you understand what's happening and stop feeding the reaction with panic and shame. The same tone that used to hook you for hours becomes a moment you can move through. The recovery gets quicker. The sting still happens, but it doesn't linger in the same way.

And then there are other triggers. The ones that don't respond as quickly. The ones that feel like they come from deeper inside you because they don't just activate stress—they shake your sense of self. They don't feel like a momentary reaction so much as a full internal weather system.

This is where people often get discouraged and assume they're doing it wrong. But this isn't about doing it wrong. It's about layers. Some trigger responses are more like sparks that catch when your baseline is already elevated. Others are tied to older learning about safety and connection, and those don't shift just because you've become more self-aware. They shift when the nervous system gathers enough lived experience that the old rule is no longer necessary.

Let's recap something we've already touched on, because it matters here. Beneath your conscious awareness, your nervous system is always scanning. It reads cues faster than you can interpret them: tone, expression, pace, uncertainty, and the subtle feeling of connection tightening or loosening. This is why you can feel something in your body before you've had time to think. Your system has already made a prediction.

When something feels threatening, the nervous system doesn't store it neatly as a story. It stores it as learning. It becomes a template: "When this happens, do this." A tone like that means danger. A silence like that means abandonment. Disappointment like that means punishment is coming. Conflict like that means connection is at risk. Sometimes you remember the original experience clearly. Sometimes you don't. Either way, your body remembers the pattern, and it will run the program as soon as it detects a cue that resembles the old one.

This is why some triggers feel bigger than the present moment. What you're reacting to is not only the current situation. You're reacting to the nervous system's prediction of what this kind of situation usually means. The present might be a two out of ten, but the template it activates was built in moments that felt like an eight. From the body's perspective, reacting hard makes sense because the body is trying to prevent a repeat.

Not all trigger responses are created equal. Some are primarily about current stress. When your baseline is raised—you're tired, overloaded, stretched thin—you have less buffer. You're closer to the edge. In that state, small sparks become big fires. As you lower your baseline and strengthen your regulation skills, those sparks lose fuel. You still feel them, but you don't spiral in the same way. You return more quickly, and you stop turning every activation into a crisis.

Other trigger responses aren't just sparks. They're wired in as protective reflexes, usually because they're tied to older learning about safety and connection. These are the moments where your body reacts as if something vital is at stake. You might know intellectually that you're not in danger, but your system behaves as if you are, because the old rule isn't a belief. It's a prediction. It sounds like "If I'm criticized, I'm unsafe." "If I disappoint someone, I'll be rejected." "If someone is upset, I'm in trouble." "If I need too much, I'll lose connection." These rules don't change just because you argue with them. They change when your nervous system experiences enough moments where the feared outcome doesn't happen, and you stay present long enough for that to register.

This is also where people often try to push too hard. They think the way through a trigger is to force themselves to tolerate the hardest version of it until it stops hurting. But overwhelm doesn't build capacity. Overwhelm usually reinforces the old rule because your nervous system doesn't learn "I can handle this" when it's flooded. It learns "See? It was too much."

Capacity builds differently. It builds when you can touch the edge of an old reaction and stay connected to yourself. That doesn't mean calm. It means connected. It means you can notice the flashpoint and soften one thing. You can pause before responding. You can step away and actually come back. You can name what's happening internally without collapsing into it: "This is old learning, and my nervous system is protecting me."

Those moments might feel small, but they matter because they create new outcomes. Each time you return without escalating, each time you repair instead of disappear, each time you meet your own activation without self-attack, you teach your nervous system something it can actually use: We can feel this and still have choices. That is how old templates update: not with one heroic breakthrough but with many small returns.

This is also why shame is such a problem here. When a reaction feels disproportionate, people often punish themselves for it. They treat it as embarrassing, immature, or irrational. But disproportion is often a clue. It can signal that the present moment has touched an older layer of emotion, from a time when you had fewer options and your system needed to protect you quickly. Compassion doesn't excuse harmful behavior. It simply removes the self-attack so the nervous system can learn something new.

And sometimes, despite all the skills in this book, you'll notice a trigger pattern that stays sticky. It keeps flaring no matter how much you regulate, rest, repair, and try again. In those cases, deeper support can be genuinely helpful because you're working with learning that formed when you couldn't change the environment, only your adaptation to it. There is no prize for doing everything alone. There's only the question "What helps your nervous system feel safe enough to update?"

The thread through all of this is simple. You're not trying to delete your past. You're teaching your nervous system a new truth: The present is not the past. And you teach it the same way the old rule was learned: not through explanation, but through lived experience, repetition, and return.

Part 6: When You're Triggered, and You Can't Fix It Yet – How to Hold the Moment Without Making It Worse

One of the most frustrating parts of being human is this: Sometimes you can see the pattern, you can name the trigger, you can even feel the old rule running . . . and you still can't change it in the moment. It's not that you're weak; it's because triggers don't always resolve on the timeline your brain would prefer. Sometimes the conversation still needs to happen. The relationship is still messy. The situation is still uncertain. The wound is still tender. You're doing your best, but your nervous system is not ready to "update the template" today.

This is where a lot of people get stuck, because they assume that if they can't fix it, they're failing. So they push harder. They explain more, overthink, over-apologize, over-function, or shut down and disappear. They try to force resolution because the uncertainty feels unbearable.

But there is another option. You can hold the moment without solving it yet.

Holding the moment is not passive. It's active containment. It's staying on your own side while your nervous system is still activated, so the reaction doesn't become a chain reaction. It's recognizing that you may not be able to fix the situation right now, but you can stop it from turning into more damage.

The first move is often internal: lower the stakes. When you're triggered, your nervous system tries to turn the situation into a referendum on your safety, worth, or belonging. It starts building a story that says, "This means something huge." So one of the most stabilizing things you can do is reduce the emotional stakes in your own system, even if the issue itself is important. You're not denying reality. You're preventing your nervous system from turning discomfort into catastrophe. Sometimes the most regulating message is simply "This is hard, but it is not an emergency, and I don't have to solve it right now."

From there, you can use a pause that protects connection. A lot of people hear "pause" and think it means avoidance, but a good pause isn't disappearing. It's buying time for your nervous system to come down so you don't create regret. You can name the pause in a way that reassures the relationship: "I want to respond well; can I have a minute?" "I'm feeling activated; let me come back to this." "I'm not ready to talk about this properly yet, but I will be." Those sentences do two things at once. They create space, and they communicate that you're not abandoning the conversation; you're regulating.

When you can't fix it yet, it helps to aim for a minimum effective response, the smallest response that prevents escalation. Your job is not to deliver the perfect answer in the heat of activation. Your job is to stop the situation from getting worse while your nervous system comes down. That might mean saying less. It might mean giving one clear sentence and then pausing. It might mean choosing silence intentionally, not as punishment but as containment. The trap is continuing to talk while your nervous system is climbing, because the more activated you are, the more likely you are to create fallout that you then have to repair.

Another crucial skill is separating the trigger from the decision. In activation, your nervous system pushes for immediate action: immediate replies, immediate conclusions, immediate reassurance, immediate control. But a triggered state is not a good time to make decisions, especially relational ones. A clean boundary with yourself is "I am allowed to feel this without acting on it." You can feel the panic without sending the message. You can feel the anger without delivering the speech. You can feel the shame without apologizing for existing. You can feel the urge to run without burning the bridge. Feelings are data. They are not instructions.

In some moments, the deepest relief doesn't come from resolving the issue. It comes from containing it, so it stops consuming you. Containment means "This is real, and it's not taking over my whole life today." Sometimes that containment is physical: stepping outside, washing your face, sitting down and letting the chair hold you, pressing your feet into the floor. Sometimes it's structural: deciding you'll return to this at a set time instead of letting it dominate the entire day, writing one note that says, "This matters, we'll revisit," and then closing the loop for now. Sometimes it's relational: stating that you care, but you can't do it right now, and you will come back.

One thing that often keeps a trigger response alive in the background is rehearsing. When you're activated and you can't fix it yet, your mind will often start running simulations: what you should have said, what they might say next, how to make them understand, how to win the case. It feels productive, but it usually keeps your body in threat mode. It's like throwing petrol on a fire while telling yourself you're trying to put it out. So instead of rehearsing, come back to the body and the present; shift location, change posture, lengthen one exhale, let your eyes move around the room. Give your nervous system a cue that you are here, now, and not under attack.

And if the trigger involved another person and you didn't handle it perfectly, the next best moment is repair, but repair from the CEO, not the Caveman. A clean repair doesn't require groveling or a long explanation. It can be simple: "I was activated earlier, and I'm sorry for how that landed." "I care about this, and I want to come back to it when I can hear you properly." "I'm working on responding rather than reacting." The point is not self-punishment. The point is restoring safety and connection so the pattern doesn't harden.

When you practice this, something shifts at a baseline level. Your nervous system learns that it doesn't have to escalate to be safe and it doesn't have to collapse to keep connection. It learns that a pause isn't abandonment and that you can feel something intense and still be okay. That learning reduces the urgency that drives so many trigger cycles, and it creates the conditions for deeper updating later.

Sometimes the bravest thing you can do in a trigger is not to solve it. It's to stay with yourself until you can come back as you.

Closing: Triggers Are Proof of Learning

Being triggered can make it feel like you've been pulled out of your own life. One moment you're here, in the present, and the next you're braced, defending, disappearing, or spiraling, and you can't quite explain why it hit so hard. When that happens, it's easy to turn the experience into a story about your character: that you're fragile, irrational, too sensitive, or somehow failing at the work.

But getting triggered is not proof of weakness. It's proof of learning. It's your nervous system doing what it was designed to do: protect you through pattern recognition. The problem isn't that your system reacts. The problem is that it sometimes reacts to the present as if it were the past, using an old template that was built in different circumstances, with fewer options and higher stakes.

Once you understand that, the task becomes clearer and kinder. You stop trying to get rid of triggers through willpower or perfect behavior, and you start reading them as information. You learn your trigger signature, not so you can judge it, but so you can recognize it sooner. You stabilize the body first because you understand that the nervous system needs evidence of safety before it can take in perspective. And when you don't handle a moment perfectly, you focus on repair because repair is one of the fastest ways your nervous system learns that activation doesn't have to end in disconnection.

Some triggers will soften quickly as your baseline steadies and your system gets more practice returning. Others will take longer because they're tied to deeper rules about safety, belonging, worth, and connection. Either way, the direction stays the same: You're building a new relationship with your own activation. You're learning to hold the moment without escalating it, to pause without abandoning, and to come back without shame.

This is what progress actually looks like. Not the disappearance of triggers but the shortening of their grip over time. Not the perfect response but the ability to return. Not a life where you never get pulled but a growing trust that when you do, you can find your way back to yourself.

Chapter 9

BOUNDARIES, COMMUNICATION, AND NERVOUS SYSTEM-SAFETY IN RELATIONSHIPS

When Calm Becomes a Team Sport

There's a particular kind of moment that can make even the most grounded person feel wobbly.

You walk into a room, and the tension is already there. Nobody has said anything yet, but you can feel it in the air. Someone is clipped. Someone is withdrawn. Someone is "fine" in that way that makes your stomach tighten before your mind has caught up.

And then you notice your own body starting to match it. Your shoulders lift, your breath rises, your attention narrows. Your mind begins scanning for the threat: What did I miss? What did I do? What's about to happen?

It's a very human reaction.

One of the most helpful truths about calm is also one of the least talked about: Calm isn't only something you generate inside yourself. Calm is something that happens *between* people. Nervous systems are social. They read each other constantly, and they influence each other whether we mean them to or not.

That's why a grounded person can make you exhale without saying much. It's also why one tense message can hijack your whole morning, and why some conversations feel exhausting before they've even started.

Relationships are where calm gets tested in a very specific way. When you're alone, you can control inputs, pace, and environment. When you're with other people, you're in a moving system. There are tones, reactions, misunderstandings, histories, and needs colliding in real time. So if you've ever felt like your regulation skills disappear the moment someone else is involved, that doesn't mean you're doing it wrong. It usually means you've entered a space where your nervous system has more to read.

Part 1: Why Calm Isn't Just Internal

Most people think calm is a solo project. You build skills, you practice awareness, you learn to steady yourself, and over time, you become more resilient. That matters, and it's exactly what you've been building throughout this book.

But relationships add another layer, because relationships aren't just two minds talking. They're two nervous systems interacting. And nervous systems are contagious in subtle ways that you've probably experienced a thousand times without naming it.

You can feel your body relax when someone speaks gently to you. You can feel your chest tighten when someone's voice sharpens, even if the words are reasonable. You can walk into a space and sense that something is off before anyone explains what's happening. That isn't you being "too sensitive." It's your system doing what it's designed to do: scanning for cues of safety and danger.

We've already talked about this scanning process earlier in the book. What matters here is that it doesn't only happen inside you. It happens in the space between you and other people. Your nervous system is reading tone, pace, expression, proximity, unpredictability, and the subtle question underneath so many interactions: "Is connection stable right now, or is it at risk?"

When connection feels at risk, even in small ways, your nervous system doesn't wait for a rational debate. It mobilizes. It braces. It tries to protect you.

And the ways it protects you are often misunderstood. You might become defensive, controlling, or sharp. You might rush to fix the tension. You might over-explain. You might go quiet and disappear inside yourself. You might become hyper-agreeable and try to smooth everything over. These aren't personality defects. They're protection strategies that usually formed for a reason.

This is also where boundaries stop being a "communication skill" and start being what they really are: a safety skill.

A boundary is what allows your nervous system to stay connected without going into protection mode. It's the difference between being honest and bracing. Between having needs and feeling guilty for having them. Between taking space and disappearing. When boundaries are clear, your system doesn't have to scream to be heard. It doesn't have to explode or collapse. It can stay online.

There's a word for the way nervous systems affect each other: co-regulation. You don't need the term to understand the experience. It's what happens when someone's steadiness helps you settle. It's also what happens when someone else's anxiety or irritability quietly winds your system up.

Co-regulation is why communication is never just about content. It's about the state underneath the content. It's why "just talk it out" sometimes works beautifully and sometimes makes everything worse. If two people are in a regulated state, even hard conversations can go well. If one or both people are in survival mode, the exact same conversation can become a mess.

This is the trap many relationships fall into: trying to solve relational problems from Red.

Red doesn't do nuance. Red doesn't do curiosity. Red doesn't do "maybe I misunderstood." In Red, a request can feel like criticism. A delay can feel like rejection. A tone can feel like a threat. And because both nervous systems are scanning for danger, both people start responding to the worst interpretation of each other.

That's why the words often aren't the real problem. The state is.

A lot of relationship pain comes from good people trying to do relationship admin while their nervous systems are flooded. The goal isn't to become perfect at communication. The goal is to stop asking your worst version of you to lead the conversation.

And this is where "safety" needs a quick definition because people often confuse it with "pleasant." Safety isn't the absence of conflict. Safety is the presence of repair. It's being able to be honest without punishment. It's being able to have limits without losing love. It's knowing that a hard moment doesn't automatically mean disconnection.

When relationships become safer at a nervous system level, calm becomes easier. Safer doesn't mean simpler, but your body doesn't have to stay braced in order to stay connected.

Part 2: Boundaries vs. Walls
The Difference Between Protection and Connection

When people hear the word "boundary," they often picture something harsh.

A stiff no. A confrontation. A hard line in the sand. Something you say when you've had enough.

And sometimes boundaries do need to be firm. But if boundaries only show up when you're already at breaking point, they tend to come out in a way that doesn't feel like you. They can come out sharp, apologetic, over-explained, or flooded with emotion because the boundary isn't coming from your values. It's coming from your nervous system trying to survive.

This is one reason boundaries get a bad reputation. People confuse boundaries with walls.

A boundary is something you set so you can stay in relationship without losing yourself.

A wall is something you put up when relationship no longer feels safe.

From the outside, they can look similar. Both might involve distance. Both might involve saying no. Both might involve stopping a pattern. But the internal experience is different, and that difference matters because your nervous system can feel it.

A boundary is connected.

Even when it's firm, it still carries the signal "I'm here. I care. And this is what I need."

A wall is protective.

It carries a different signal: "I'm not safe. I'm done. I'm out."

Neither is "wrong." If something is genuinely unsafe, walls can be necessary. But many people build walls because they don't know how to set boundaries early enough. They don't know how to protect themselves without disconnecting.

So let's make this practical.

WHY BOUNDARIES FEEL HARD (EVEN WHEN YOU KNOW YOU NEED THEM)

Most people don't struggle with boundaries because they can't think of the right sentence. They struggle because boundaries touch the deepest relational fears.

> Fear of being seen as difficult.
> Fear of disappointing someone.
> Fear of conflict.
> Fear of being rejected.
> Fear of being "too much."
> Fear of being punished for having needs.

When those fears are active, your nervous system will default to whatever strategy used to keep you safest.

For some people, that strategy is fawning. They over-explain, over-accommodate, soften the boundary until it disappears, and then resent the other person for not reading their mind.

For others, it's freezing. They go quiet, avoid the conversation, let the boundary be crossed, and then feel ashamed for "not standing up for themselves."

For others, it's fighting. They wait until they're full, then explode. The boundary comes out like a weapon because it's arriving late and loaded.

For others, it's fleeing. They distance. They withdraw. They end relationships quickly rather than risk the discomfort of negotiation.

All of those are understandable. They're also exhausting.

And they all come from the same place: a nervous system trying to keep connection, safety, and belonging at the same time.

The Nervous System's Purpose of a Boundary

A boundary is not primarily about controlling someone else's behavior.

A boundary is about creating enough safety in *you* that you can stay present.

It's a signal to your nervous system that you are paying attention. That you will protect your time, your energy, your values, your body, your emotional space. That you don't have to go into collapse or aggression to be safe.

In that sense, boundaries are baseline-builders. They reduce the background load your nervous system carries in relationships. They prevent the slow leak of overgiving and overfunctioning that eventually turns into resentment or shutdown.

This is why boundaries are so linked to calm.

If you never say no, your nervous system has to brace.

If you never name what you need, your system has to keep scanning.

If you keep tolerating what doesn't work for you, your system will eventually protect you in a less elegant way.

A boundary is the elegant way.

THE "BOUNDARY SWEET SPOT"

Most people swing between two extremes.

On one side is over-accommodation. You say yes when you mean no. You stay polite while your body is screaming. You try to be easy to be around, and you end up feeling invisible or drained.

On the other side is rigid protection. You shut down. You cut people off. You become blunt. You go cold. You build a wall because you don't know how to hold a boundary without losing connection.

The sweet spot is in the middle.

It's firm and kind.

It protects you without punishing the other person.

It tells the truth without escalating.

It's not "nice." It's clear.

And it's rarely a speech. It's usually a simple statement that you repeat without defending it.

That's where calm shows up in boundaries. Not in perfect wording, but in the state underneath the wording.

What It Feels like When a Boundary Is Coming from Red

Here's a quick check-in that can save you a lot of regret.

If you feel urgency, tightness, or a desire to "make them understand," you're probably close to Red.

When a boundary comes from Red, it tends to sound like:

- a long explanation
- a harsh statement you later feel guilty about
- an apology wrapped around the truth
- a list of evidence and examples
- a "final straw" speech

And even if the content is valid, it often lands badly because the nervous system signal underneath it is threat.

This is why the first boundary skill is often a pause, so you can choose the state you want to set it from.

If you can step from Red back toward Yellow, even slightly, the boundary will come out cleaner. It will sound more like you. It will be easier to hold.

What It Feels like When a Boundary Is Coming from Green

When you're in Green, a boundary doesn't need to be dramatic.

It's just information.

It's "This works for me" and "This doesn't."

It doesn't require a courtroom case. It doesn't require the other person to agree. It doesn't require you to be perfectly calm. It just requires enough steadiness that you can say the thing and stay with yourself.

Green boundaries tend to be shorter.

They're specific.

And they leave space for relationship.

They sound like:

> "I can't do that."
> "I'm not available for that kind of conversation right now."
> "That doesn't work for me."
> "I need some time to think about it."
> "I'm happy to talk about this, but not like this."

Notice what's missing:

No attack

No over-explaining.

No collapse.

Just clarity. And clarity is regulating because when you become someone your nervous system can rely on to set limits, your system doesn't have to keep escalating to get your attention.

Part 3: Minimum Effective Boundaries How to Say It Simply, Hold It Steadily, and Stay Connected

Most boundary advice falls into one of two categories. It's either too vague to be useful ("just communicate your needs"), or it's so scripted it feels like you're reading from a counselling worksheet while your nervous system is on fire.

What people actually need, especially in real life, is something simpler. A boundary that works in the moment. A boundary you can remember when your capacity is low. A boundary that protects you without escalating the situation or turning you into someone you don't want to be.

That's what I mean by a minimum effective boundary.

A minimum effective boundary is the smallest, clearest statement that protects what matters without over-explaining or over-negotiating. It's not the perfect sentence. It's the sentence that prevents the situation from getting worse and gives your nervous system enough safety to stay present.

This matters because when people struggle with boundaries, it's rarely because they don't know what they want. It's because their nervous system thinks the boundary will cost them something: approval, belonging, connection, peace, or safety. So they soften it until it disappears, or they delay it until it comes out sharp. Minimum effective boundaries help you avoid both extremes.

The Three Ingredients of a Boundary That Holds

A boundary that holds usually has three ingredients: clarity, brevity, and follow-through.

Clarity means you're not hinting. You're not hoping the other person will infer what you mean. You're saying what works and what doesn't.

Brevity means you're not building a case. Long explanations often sound like negotiation, even when you don't mean them that way. They give the other person something to debate, and they keep your nervous system stuck in justification mode.

Follow-through means you're willing to act on what you've said. Not in a punitive way, but in a steady way. Because a boundary without follow-through becomes a request. And if the pattern has been entrenched for a long time, requests often get ignored.

When these three ingredients are present, boundaries feel calmer because your nervous system can feel you taking your own side.

What Minimum Effective Boundaries Sound Like

Most minimum effective boundaries fall into a few simple shapes. You can think of them as "sentence stems" you can adapt to your life, rather than scripts you have to memorize.

One shape is a clear no:

> "I can't do that."
> "That doesn't work for me."
> "I'm not available for that."

Another shape is a limit around time or capacity:

> "I can do X, but not Y."
> "I can do that this week, but not today."
> "I have twenty minutes, then I need to stop."

Another shape is a limit around tone or process:

> "I'm happy to talk about this, but not like this."
> "I want to keep talking, and I need us to slow down."
> "I'm going to take a break and come back when we're both calmer."

Another shape is a boundary around access:

> "I'm not going to respond to messages after 8 p.m."
> "I'm not discussing this at work."
> "I'm not comfortable sharing that."

Notice what these have in common. They're not attacks. They're not moral judgements. They're not diagnoses. They're simple statements of what you will do, what you won't do, and what you need in order to stay present.

And here's the part many people miss: A boundary doesn't have to convince the other person. It only has to be clear enough that *you* can hold it.

The Nervous System Skill: Tolerating the Wobble

Even when you state the boundary perfectly, there's often a moment afterward that feels uncomfortable. The other person might pause. They might look disappointed, push back, go quiet, or question you. They might do nothing at all.

This is the moment when many people abandon themselves.

Although they might mean the boundary, their nervous system can't tolerate the relational wobble that follows. That wobble can feel like danger if your system has learned that disapproval leads to rejection or conflict leads to punishment.

So the real boundary work is often not the sentence.

It's staying with yourself in that moment afterward.

It's letting the wobble be there without rushing to repair it by undoing your boundary. It's noticing the urge to over-explain, to appease, to justify, to soften, and choosing instead to breathe, slow down, and let the discomfort pass through.

You can't control how someone reacts to your boundary, but you can control whether you abandon yourself when they react.

And this is where calm becomes visible in relationships. Calm is not stating boundaries without a nervous system response. Calm is being able to feel the response and hold the boundary anyway.

What to Do When Someone Pushes Back

If you have a history of over-explaining, this will be important. People often push back not because your boundary is unreasonable but because it's new. It changes the usual pattern. And patterns don't like change.

When someone pushes back, the temptation is to defend yourself or produce more evidence. But defending usually escalates, and evidence usually turns the boundary into a debate.

A minimum effective response here is repetition.

You calmly restate the boundary in slightly different words, without adding new information.

For example:

> "I hear that you're disappointed. I still can't do that."
> "I understand you want an answer right now. I'm going to think about it and come back to you."
> "I'm not willing to keep talking while we're speaking like this. Let's pause."

This is not cold. It's steady. It's you staying in connection without moving the line.

If the pushback continues, follow-through is what protects you. That might mean ending the conversation, stepping away, changing the subject, or simply disengaging. Not in a dramatic way. In a calm, predictable way that tells your nervous system, "We mean what we say."

Boundaries That Protect the Relationship

It's worth saying this clearly, because a lot of people worry that boundaries will damage relationships.

Unclear boundaries damage relationships.

Resentment damages relationships.

Silence damages relationships.

Explosions damage relationships.

A clean boundary, said early enough, often protects the relationship from all of that. It prevents the build-up. It prevents the blow-up. It keeps you out of the cycle where you overgive until you can't, then withdraw.

A boundary is not a rejection of the other person. It's an act of care for the relationship and for yourself because it creates the conditions where you can stay present without going into protection mode.

And when you practice minimum effective boundaries over time, something shifts quietly. Your nervous system learns that you can have needs and still belong. You can disappoint someone and still be safe. You can say no and still be connected. You can be clear without being cruel.

That learning is a form of calm.

In the next part, we'll look at what happens when boundaries are tested in the moments that matter most: conflict, emotional intensity, and the situations where your old patterns are most likely to take over.

PART 4: WHEN BOUNDARIES GET TESTED CONFLICT, INTENSITY, AND STAYING GROUNDED WITHOUT COLLAPSING OR GOING TO WAR

Most boundaries are easy in theory.

They're much harder in the exact moment you need them. The moment someone is disappointed. The moment the tone changes. The moment you feel the old urge to keep the peace, prove your point, withdraw, or fight back.

This is where boundaries stop being a concept and become a nervous system practice.

When intensity rises, your body will try to protect you in familiar ways. If your default is to over-function, you'll feel the urge to explain and smooth things over. If your default is to shut down, you'll feel yourself go blank or quiet. If your default is to fight, you'll feel the heat and the sharpness. If your default is to flee, you'll feel the urge to escape the whole conversation.

None of those responses is random. They're your system reaching for the strategy that once helped you stay safe.

The goal here isn't to erase your pattern. The goal is to recognize it early enough that it doesn't drive the whole interaction.

The real test: Can you stay in connection while you hold the line?

A boundary is easy to say when the other person agrees.

A boundary gets tested when the other person doesn't like it.

That's when the nervous system starts interpreting the pushback as danger: disapproval, conflict, distance, rejection. That's when people abandon themselves and move the line, or they harden into a wall because they don't know how to stay connected.

So here's a simple reframe that helps: A boundary is not something you set once. It's something you hold.

Holding is the skill.

Holding is staying steady through the wobble, through the disappointment, through the silence, through the raised eyebrows, through the "seriously?" energy. You don't enjoy tension, but your nervous system needs to learn that tension is survivable.

This is why boundaries are so linked to calm. They train you to stay present in mild relational discomfort without flipping into protection mode.

What Conflict Does to the Nervous System

Conflict activates threat circuitry fast, even in relationships that are fundamentally safe. A change in tone, a perceived criticism, an unmet expectation, these are the kinds of cues the nervous system treats as relational risk.

And once that risk is detected, the body changes.

Breath rises. Muscles tighten. Attention narrows. Your mind starts building a case. You stop listening for understanding and start listening for threat. The conversation becomes less about the actual issue and more about who feels safe, who feels heard, and who feels respected.

This is why conflict can feel so disproportionate. It's not just about the content. It's about what the nervous system thinks the content *means*.

If you want to communicate well in conflict, the first goal isn't to say the perfect thing. It's to keep your nervous system online enough that you can stay in the conversation without turning it into a fight-or-flight event.

The "Yellow zone" boundary is your best friend.

In Chapter 7, we talked about Yellow as the zone where you're activated but still reachable. That applies here too. Most relationship damage happens when people wait until they're in Red to set the boundary.

In Yellow, the boundary can be smaller and cleaner. It can be said with less emotion. It can be held with less force.

In Red, the boundary becomes an explosion, a shutdown, or a dramatic exit. Even if the boundary is valid, it tends to land like a threat because it's being delivered by a threatened nervous system.

So one of the most effective relationship habits you can build is this: Set boundaries earlier than you think you need to.

Say the small thing before it becomes the big thing.

Name the need before it becomes resentment.

Ask for a change in tone before you're flooded.

Pause before you're sharp.

This is not about being overly sensitive. It's about being smart with your nervous system.

Boundaries in the Hard Moments

Let's bring this down to real life, because this is where people need it most.

WHEN SOMEONE IS ESCALATING:

If the other person is getting louder, sharper, or more intense, your nervous system will either rise to meet them or collapse to get away. The minimum effective boundary here is usually about pace and tone.

You might say, "I want to talk about this, and I need us to slow down." Or, "I'm not okay to keep going while we're speaking like this." If it continues, the follow-through is a pause: "I'm going to take a break and come back."

Notice the difference between a pause and a punishment. A pause is specific and grounded. It says you're returning. A punishment is vague and disconnecting. It says, "Good luck guessing when I'll be back."

WHEN YOU FEEL YOURSELF GOING BLANK:

For many people, the hardest boundary is not saying no. It's naming that they are no longer able to think or speak clearly. Freeze is real, and it can feel humiliating if you don't understand it.

A boundary here can be as simple as "I can't think clearly right now. I need a minute." Or "I'm starting to shut down. I want to keep talking, but I need a reset first." That is not weakness. That is skill. It prevents you from nodding along to something you don't agree with just to escape the moment.

WHEN THE URGE TO OVER-EXPLAIN KICKS IN:

Over-explaining is usually a safety behavior. It's your nervous system trying to prevent disapproval by being perfectly understood. The problem is that it often backfires. The more you explain, the more it sounds like negotiation, and the more the conversation spirals.

So in these moments, the boundary is with yourself. It's choosing brevity even when your body wants to talk.

You can say the line, then stop. You can let silence do its job. You can tolerate the wobble without filling it.

When the conversation becomes a courtroom:

This is the moment when you both start collecting evidence. Who said what. Who started it. Who always does this. Who is the "reasonable" one. This is a sign the nervous system has switched into threat mode and is searching for control.

A boundary here is often about returning to the actual aim. You can say, "I don't want this to turn into a debate about who's right. I want us to understand each other." Or more simply, "I'm not doing the blame version of this."

If the courtroom energy keeps rising, pause. The relationship does not need a verdict. It needs nervous systems that can hear each other.

The strongest boundary is sometimes not a sentence.

Sometimes the strongest boundary is changing what you do next.

> You stop replying to messages that come in hot.
> You don't engage in the conversation when you're flooded.
> You leave the room and come back.
> You don't keep negotiating after you've said no.

This is what follow-through looks like. Calm, predictable action. Not punishment. Not drama. Just consistency. Because the nervous system trusts consistency. It settles when it knows what happens next.

PART 5: COMMUNICATION THAT CREATES SAFETY
HOW TO SAY HARD THINGS WITHOUT LIGHTING THE FUSE

Most people think communication is about getting the words right.

So when a conversation goes badly, they replay it and look for the sentence that ruined everything. They tell themselves they should have been clearer, calmer, more persuasive, more reasonable. They search for the perfect way to say it so the other person won't react.

But communication doesn't land in the mind first.

It lands in the nervous system.

Long before someone processes your logic, their body has already registered your tone, your pace, your facial expression, and whether you feel like a threat or a teammate. And your body is registering the same in them. That's why two people can have the exact same conversation, with the exact same words, and it can feel either safe and productive or tense and explosive, depending on the state each person is in.

This is what makes communication in relationships so tricky. It isn't just about what you mean. It's about what the other nervous system can receive.

So instead of starting with "What should I say?" it helps to start with a different question: "What signal am I sending right now?"

It is the signal that sets the tone of the entire interaction. If your nervous system is tense, urgent, or braced, the signal will often be threat, even if your words are kind. If your nervous system is steady, the signal will often be safety, even if the message is hard.

The Three Safety Signals That Change Everything

There are many communication skills you can learn, but most of them sit on top of three simple safety signals. When these are present, hard conversations become easier to have. When they're missing, even small conversations can escalate.

The first signal is **pace**.

When people feel threatened, they speed up. They interrupt. They pile on points. They talk over each other. They push for resolution. Speed communicates urgency, and urgency can feel like danger to a nervous system that is already activated.

Slowing down is not just a social nicety. It's a regulation strategy. It gives both nervous systems time to stay online.

The second signal is **tone**.

Tone is one of the fastest ways the nervous system decides whether you are safe. A sharp tone can land like an attack even when the content is reasonable. A warm tone can lower threat even when you're saying no.

This is why "I'm fine" can be terrifying, and "We need to talk" can make someone sweat instantly. The nervous system hears the tone underneath the words and reacts accordingly.

The third signal is **predictability**.

Predictability doesn't mean you never change your mind. It means you communicate in a way that the other person can follow. You don't disappear mid-conversation. You don't punish with silence. You don't escalate without warning. You don't say, "It's fine," and then explode two days later. You create continuity.

Predictability is safety.

When these three signals are present, slower pace, steadier tone, clearer predictability, communication becomes far less threatening. Even when the content is uncomfortable, the nervous system can stay in the conversation long enough to process it.

The Communication Trap: Trying to Be Understood While You're Activated

One of the most common ways conflict escalates is simple: Someone is activated, and they keep talking.

They're not trying to be cruel. They're trying to be understood. They're trying to fix the discomfort quickly. They're trying to stop feeling unsafe.

But when you're activated, your words change. You talk faster. You say more than you mean. You become absolute. You reach for old evidence. You start using words like always and never. You go into courtroom mode. You stop listening. You start winning.

And the other nervous system hears that and reacts.

So if you take one principle from this part, let it be this: When you notice activation rising, less is often safer.

If you choose not to flood the conversation with chemistry, you give yourself a chance to come down before you say something you can't unsay.

This is where the pause becomes a communication skill, not just a regulation tool.

A pause done well can sound like "I want to talk about this, but I'm getting activated. I need a few minutes." That sentence alone can prevent hours of damage because it names what's happening without blaming, and it creates a predictable plan for return.

How to Say Hard Things Without Turning Them into a Threat

There's a simple structure that tends to create safety even when the content is hard. It's not a script. It's a shape.

You can think of it as **name, own, ask**.

You name what you're noticing, without accusation.

You own your experience, without making the other person responsible for your feelings.

And you ask for what you need, clearly.

For example:

"I noticed I felt tense after that conversation. I think I interpreted your tone as frustration. I want to check what you meant, and I want to talk about how we handle it when we're both tired."

Or:

"I'm feeling overloaded this week. I know I've been snappier than I want to be. I need us to keep evenings lighter for a few days, and I'll tell you when I'm back in range."

Or:

"I care about this, and I'm not willing to keep talking when we're both escalating. I'm going to take twenty minutes and come back."

Notice what that does. It keeps the nervous system signal as "teammate" rather than "enemy." It reduces defensiveness because you're not launching blame. And it creates predictability, because you're being clear about what happens next.

The power move: Reflect before you defend.

In many conflicts, the underlying problem is not the topic. It's that people don't feel heard.

When someone feels unheard, their nervous system escalates. They repeat themselves more loudly. They sharpen their words. They push harder. They become more intense because intensity is the body's attempt to get impact.

This is why one of the most regulating things you can do in conflict is to reflect before you defend.

That doesn't mean you agree. It means you show the other nervous system that you got the message.

You can reflect in one sentence:

> "I hear that you felt dismissed."
> "I can see why that landed badly."
> "It makes sense that you're upset."

Those sentences aren't admissions of guilt. They're safety cues. They tell the other nervous system, "I'm with you enough to listen."

Once someone feels heard, the intensity often drops. And once intensity drops, problem-solving becomes possible again.

Communication That Builds Trust Over Time

Good communication isn't just about what you say in the moment. It's about the patterns you build over time.

Do you come back after you pause, or do you disappear?

Do you repair after a hard moment, or do you pretend it didn't happen?

Do you speak the small truth early, or do you store it until it becomes resentment?

Do you set boundaries with clarity, or do you hint and hope?

Trust is built through predictability. Your nervous system trusts people who do what they say. Other nervous systems do too.

This is why the goal isn't perfect communication. The goal is safe communication, communication that keeps both people's nervous systems online enough to stay in relationship while you navigate real life.

Part 6: When the Other Person Doesn't Play Along Staying Steady When Someone Escalates, Shuts Down, or Pushes Your Line

It's one thing to practice boundaries and safer communication when the other person is also regulated, reasonable, and invested in doing it well.

It's another thing entirely when they're not.

Real relationships include people who escalate when they're stressed, people who go quiet when they feel criticized, people who push back when you set a limit, and people who use guilt or intensity to try to get their way. Sometimes this happens because they're manipulative. More often, it happens because they're activated and don't know what else to do.

Either way, the result is the same: Your nervous system gets pulled.

And if you're someone who's been trained to manage other people's emotions, this is where your calm skills will be tested hardest. You'll feel the familiar urge to smooth it over, fix it, explain more, or give in just to make the tension stop.

So this part is about what to do when the other nervous system is not cooperating, and you still want to stay on your own side.

It starts with one simple truth: You are only responsible for your side of the interaction. You can create safety signals, offer clarity, and stay regulated as best you can, but you cannot regulate someone else *for* them. You can invite a healthier pattern. You can't force it.

That's not pessimistic. It's freeing.

When Someone Escalates

Escalation can look like raised volume, sharpness, sarcasm, rapid-fire points, blaming, or the sense that the conversation is speeding out of control.

The temptation is to match the energy. To defend, argue, prove, correct, win.

But escalation is a state problem, not a logic problem. If you meet it with more words, you often pour fuel on it.

So the goal is to reduce threat signals, reduce complexity, and create a predictable boundary.

That can sound like "I want to talk about this, but I'm not willing to do it while we're escalating." Or "I'm going to pause and come back in twenty minutes."

Then the follow-through matters. If you say you're pausing, pause. Don't keep engaging in the heat. Don't fire one more sentence on the way out. Your nervous system will want that last shot. Resist it. The steadiness is what creates safety.

If you can, anchor your body as you do it. Slow the pace. Lower your volume. Soften your face. That's not about being polite. It's about not triggering the other nervous system further.

And if the other person keeps chasing the fight, you don't have to keep providing access. You can repeat the boundary and disengage. Not to punish. To contain.

When Someone Shuts Down

Shutdown can look like silence, stonewalling, leaving the room, giving one-word answers, or going emotionally blank.

People often assume shutdown is intentional manipulation. Sometimes it is. Often, it's a nervous system freeze response.

The person is overwhelmed, and their system is protecting them by going offline.

Either way, you can't force connection through shutdown. Pushing harder usually makes it worse, so the skill here is to stop trying to get resolution in the moment and instead create a bridge for return.

That can sound like "I can see you're shutting down. I don't want to force this. Let's pause and come back later." Or "I'm available to talk when you're ready, and I'm not going to keep pushing right now."

You're naming what you see without accusing. You're offering predictability. You're keeping the relationship door open without begging.

And you're also taking care of yourself because being met with silence can be deeply activating. If your system interprets silence as danger or rejection, this is where you may need to regulate yourself and remind your body that shutdown is a state, not necessarily abandonment.

When Someone Guilt-Trips or Makes You the Problem

This one can be subtle, and it can be powerful.

You set a boundary, and the other person responds with disappointment designed to make you backtrack. They imply you're selfish. They tell you you've changed. They make your limit seem unreasonable. They remind you of everything they've done for you. They get dramatic. They get wounded.

Sometimes this is deliberate. Sometimes it's just their nervous system trying to regain control and connection by pulling on an old dynamic.

Either way, the antidote is the same: Don't argue with the guilt.

Guilt is not a good place to make decisions from. If your nervous system is wired to keep connection by pleasing, guilt will feel urgent. It will make you want to fix the discomfort immediately by giving in.

So instead, you acknowledge the emotion without moving the line.

That can sound like "I hear that you're disappointed. I still can't do that." Or "I understand you don't like this. This is still my boundary."

This is where your minimum effective boundary skills really matter. You don't have to prove your boundary is valid. You just have to hold it calmly.

When Someone Keeps Pushing After You've Been Clear

Some people treat boundaries as the start of negotiation. They ask again. They reframe. They push. They test. They wait for you to get tired and cave.

If you've been the accommodating one for a long time, this is common. It doesn't automatically mean the person is awful. It often means the relationship has a pattern, and you've just changed it.

The mistake people make here is adding more and more explanation. They think that if they just explain better, the other person will finally understand. But repeated explanation often teaches the other person that pushing works because it keeps you engaged in debate.

A stronger move is calm repetition and predictable follow-through.

You restate the boundary once. Then you change what you do.

You stop responding. You end the conversation. You step away. You come back later.

This isn't harsh. It's clarity in action. It's your nervous system learning that you don't have to perform for your limits to count.

The uncomfortable truth: Sometimes the environment is the problem.

There's one more layer here that matters, and it's a hard one.

Sometimes you're not "bad at boundaries." Sometimes you're in a relationship or environment that punishes boundaries.

If every limit you set is met with rage, ridicule, withdrawal, threats, or repeated violation, your nervous system is not being dramatic when it braces. It's responding accurately.

This is where calm and safety become less about skills and more about choices. You can do a lot with regulation and communication, but there are dynamics that require distance, support, or change.

This doesn't mean you have to make drastic decisions overnight. It just means you stop gaslighting yourself. You stop treating your activation as a personal failure when it's actually a signal that something around you isn't safe.

And if you find yourself in that kind of dynamic, support matters. You shouldn't have to handle it alone.

The Bottom Line

The goal of boundaries and communication isn't to control other people. It's to stay connected to yourself while you engage with them.

Sometimes that means speaking clearly and staying soft.

Sometimes it means pausing and coming back.

Sometimes it means disengaging.

Sometimes it means holding a line through discomfort.

And sometimes it means recognizing that calm is harder to access in an environment that constantly triggers your threat system.

But in every case, the work is the same: You become someone your nervous system can trust to protect you without abandoning connection.

That's what relational calm really is.

Part 7: A Relational Reset
What to Do When You Feel the Pattern Starting

By this point, you might be thinking, "Okay, I get it. State matters. Boundaries matter. Safety matters. But what do I actually *do* when I'm in the moment, and I can feel the whole thing starting?"

The moment you need these skills is rarely a neat one. It's usually mid-text thread, mid-bedtime chaos, mid-meeting, mid-sarcastic comment, mid-eye roll. Your nervous system is already reacting, and you're trying to stop yourself from either collapsing, over-functioning, or going to war.

So here's a simple relational reset you can use when you feel the pattern begin. It's not a magical sequence. It's more like a set of moves that bring you back into choice and bring the interaction back into a safer lane.

The reset has one goal: **to reduce threat signals and increase safety signals** long enough for both nervous systems to stay online.

STEP ONE: NAME THE STATE, NOT THE STORY

When you feel the surge, your mind will usually race ahead and start building a story. They don't respect me. They always do this. I'm not safe. I'm about to be blamed. I'm going to lose connection.

In the heat of activation, those stories can feel completely true. But they're being powered by chemistry.

So the first move is to name what's happening at the level of state, not blame.

That can be as simple as admitting it internally: "I'm getting activated." Or, if it's appropriate and safe, naming it out loud without making it the other person's fault: "I can feel myself getting reactive." "I'm starting to shut down." "I want to talk about this, and my body is climbing."

That kind of naming does something important. It stops the nervous system from interpreting the surge as a crisis, and it creates a little space between you and the pattern. It also signals to the other person that you're not trying to win, you're trying to stay present.

Step Two: Slow the Pace on Purpose

Most people speed up when they feel threatened. They talk faster, explain more, stack points, push for resolution. Even if you're doing it politely, it lands as urgency.

So your next move is pace.

You slow your voice. You take one breath before you respond. You reduce the number of sentences you're using. You give the other nervous system less to brace against.

Sometimes the most regulating thing you can do is not say more. It's say less, more slowly, with a steadier tone.

This is also where a pause becomes a relationship skill, not an escape hatch. A clean pause might sound like "I want to keep talking, and I need a minute to settle." Or "I'm not going to do this fast. I'll come back to it in twenty minutes."

The key is predictability. A pause that protects connection includes a return.

Step Three: Choose the Relationship-Safe Version of the Truth

This is the part people often misunderstand. Communicating safely doesn't mean you water yourself down. It means you choose the version of the truth that doesn't light the fuse.

When you're activated, the truth tends to come out in its sharpest form. It becomes absolute. It becomes accusatory. It becomes a verdict.

So ask yourself, "What's the simplest true thing I can say that doesn't escalate?"

Instead of "You never listen to me," the relationship-safe truth might be "I don't feel heard right now."

Instead of "You're being ridiculous," it might be "I'm not able to stay with this tone."

Instead of "Fine, do whatever you want," it might be "I need some space before we keep talking."

You're not being fake. You're being skillful. You're staying connected to your truth without turning it into a threat.

Step Four: Make One Clear Request or Boundary, Then Stop

When people feel unsafe, they often throw five needs into one conversation. They try to fix the whole relationship in a single burst of intensity.

That's nervous system urgency, not strategy.

So the reset is to choose one thing. One boundary. One request. One next step.

It might be "Can we slow down?" It might be "I'm not okay with being spoken to like that." It might be "I need to take a break and come back." It might be "I need you to tell me what you meant by that."

Then you stop. You let it land.

If you keep talking after the boundary, you usually turn it into a negotiation or a courtroom case. The steadier move is to state it and hold it. That's where your minimum effective boundary skills from Part 3 earn their keep.

Step Five: If It Goes Sideways, Repair Instead of Rehearse

Even with all of this, you're still human. Sometimes you will snap. Sometimes you will go quiet. Sometimes you'll over-explain. Sometimes you'll send the text you wish you hadn't. The question isn't whether you'll ever get it wrong. The question is what you do next.

In healthy relationships, repair matters more than perfection.

Repair doesn't need to be dramatic. It can be clean and simple. "I got reactive. I'm sorry." "That came out sharper than I meant. Let me try again." "I shut down. I'm here now." "I want to understand you. Can we restart this slower?"

A repair is a safety signal. It tells the nervous system, "This relationship can handle rupture and return." That is one of the strongest predictors of long-term relational calm.

What This Looks like in Real Life

Let's make it concrete.

With a partner:

If you feel the old pattern start, the urge to defend or fix or withdraw, you can slow the pace and name the state. "I want to talk about this, and I'm getting activated. Can we pause for ten minutes and come back?" That one move prevents a lot of damage because it stops you both from fighting from Red.

With kids:

If your child is escalating and you feel your own system rising, the reset is often your body first. You lower your shoulders. You slow your voice. You become the calmest thing in the space, even if you don't feel calm inside. You can set a boundary without heat: "I'm here. I won't let you hit. I'm going to help you calm down." Kids don't borrow your lecture. They borrow your nervous system.

At work:

If you're in a meeting and someone's tone spikes you, you can use an internal reset: soften your jaw, lengthen one exhale, slow your response. Then choose the relationship-safe truth: "I want to understand the feedback. Can you say that again, more specifically?" You're not absorbing disrespect. You're steering the interaction back to a safer channel.

In each of these, the aim is the same. You're not trying to win. You're trying to stay online. You're reducing threat signals and increasing safety signals long enough for the conversation to remain human.

Closing: Stay Connected Without Abandoning Yourself

If there's one thing this chapter is trying to give you, it's this: the ability to stay connected to yourself inside your relationships.

Because calm isn't just something you practice alone on a good day. Calm is what happens when real life is happening, other nervous systems are involved, and the old patterns want to take over.

When you understand that relationships are nervous system spaces, a lot of things stop feeling personal in the unhelpful way. You stop treating your reactivity as a character flaw. You start recognizing it as a state shift. You stop hunting for perfect words and start paying attention to pace, tone, and predictability, the signals that tell the body whether it's safe enough to stay present.

Boundaries become less about being "strong" and more about being steady. Communication becomes less about persuasion and more about safety. Repair becomes more important than perfection because repair teaches your nervous system something it can actually trust: Rupture doesn't have to mean disconnection.

And yes, other people will still be other people. They will escalate. They will shut down. They will push your line. They will have their own patterns. The work isn't to control that. The work is to become someone your nervous system can rely on to stay on your own side, even when the interaction is uncomfortable.

That's what relational calm is. It's the ability to hold your truth without going cold, to set limits without going to war, and to come back to connection without abandoning yourself in the process.

In the next chapter, we'll zoom out and look at the deeper structure underneath so many of these patterns: the way your baseline, your environment, and your nervous system history shape what feels possible day to day. The more you understand what your system is working with, the less you blame yourself for not being calm on demand, and the more skilled you become at building calm that actually lasts.

Chapter 10

Building a Nervous System That Trusts You

The Long Game of Calm

Most people think calm is something you *do*.

A technique. A strategy. A trick you pull out when life gets loud.

And for a while, that's true. In the early stages, calm is very much a practice. You remember to breathe. You pause before you speak. You widen your gaze. You ground through your feet. You use the tools because you have to.

But there's another phase of this work that doesn't get talked about enough. It's the phase where calm stops being something you remember to do and starts being something your body expects. That shift isn't willpower or a personality upgrade. It's not becoming one of those "naturally calm people."

It's trust.

A nervous system that trusts you doesn't panic as quickly or escalate as fast, and it doesn't assume every discomfort is danger.

It still reacts sometimes because you're human, but it recovers more quickly, and it doesn't need to go all the way to Red to get your attention.

This is what people often mean when they say, "I feel like myself again." Not perfect or Zen or emotionally blank. Just steadier inside your own life, with more access to choice.

The tricky part is that you can't talk your nervous system into trust. You build it the same way you build trust with another person: through repetition, predictability, and repair. You show up again and again in a way that tells your body, "I'm on your side."

That's the long game of calm. And it's where the deepest change happens as your nervous system becomes less convinced that it has to brace for everything.

Part 1: Why Your Nervous System Doesn't Trust You Yet, and Why That's Not an Insult

Let's start with something that might sting a little at first but becomes incredibly freeing once you see it clearly.

If your nervous system escalates quickly, it's because it has learned, over time, that it has to.

A nervous system doesn't react based on what you *believe*. It reacts based on what it *predicts*. And prediction is built from evidence. If your life has trained your body to expect that things will pile up, that people will be unpredictable, that you'll have to hold it together, that you'll be fine right up until you're not . . . then your nervous system will behave accordingly. It will stay alert, scan constantly, and mobilize early because waiting hasn't felt safe.

This is why so many people have the experience of doing "all the right things" and still feeling activated. They read the books. They understand the concepts. They can explain the CEO and Caveman brain to other people as if they invented it. They have the tools. And yet, when it's 9 p.m. and everyone needs something, or when an email lands with the wrong tone, or when someone they love looks disappointed, the body reacts before insight can even clear its throat.

That doesn't mean the work isn't working. It means you're seeing the difference between understanding and embodiment.

Understanding is cognitive. Embodiment is biological. Biology changes slowly because it's designed to keep you alive. Your nervous system doesn't update its safety rules because you've had a good idea. It updates them when it has enough repeated experience that the new rule becomes more reliable than the old one.

The modern mind keeps bumping into this because the CEO loves insight. The CEO loves language. The CEO loves making sense of things. But the Caveman brain doesn't speak fluent logic. It speaks pattern and repetition. It says, "What happened last time?" "What usually happens?" "What tends to follow this?"

If, historically, you've pushed through exhaustion until you collapse, your body learns that the only way to get rest is crisis.

If, historically, you've ignored early signs until you blow up, your body learns that it must escalate to be noticed.

If, historically, you've over-explained in conflict to stay connected, your body learns that connection requires effort and vigilance.

If, historically, you've coped by bracing, controlling, pleasing, disappearing, performing, your body learns that those are the moves that keep you safe.

Then later, in a perfectly ordinary moment, say, in your car, in your kitchen, in a meeting, you'll find yourself wondering why you can't just "be calm."

This is why: because your nervous system is not being dramatic, it's being consistent.

And the moment you understand this, you can stop arguing with yourself. Instead of "What is wrong with me?" the question becomes "What did my system learn, and what evidence does it need now to learn something new?" That shift alone is calming because it removes the layer of shame. It replaces self-attack with strategy.

So, let's talk about what it means for a nervous system to trust you.

It doesn't mean life becomes predictable. That would be lovely, but we don't control that part. It means *you* become predictable. Your nervous system learns that when activation starts rising, you respond with support instead of criticism. It learns that when you're overloaded, you don't just keep pushing and hoping you'll magically power through. It learns that when you make a mistake, you don't punish yourself for three days. It learns that when you get triggered, you can repair. It learns that when you need something, you can name it. It learns that you will come back for yourself, even if you couldn't in the past.

This is the part people often miss, because it's not glamorous. Trust isn't built in the big moments where you practice the perfect regulation tool and feel proud of yourself; it is built in the small moments where you do something different on purpose.

You pause before you fire off the message, or you eat before you become a monster, or you step outside for sixty seconds instead of powering through until you snap. Perhaps you lower the stakes and choose the minimum effective response, or you apologize cleanly instead of spiraling into shame.

Those moments don't feel dramatic, but they are evidence. And evidence is what rewires your nervous system.

We've already touched on the idea of the "window of tolerance," and it matters here because it explains why this trust-building process takes time.

When your nervous system is within its window, you have access to more of yourself. You can think clearly enough to choose your words. You can feel discomfort without becoming it. You can stay connected while something is tense. The CEO is available, even if the Caveman is a bit noisy.

When you're outside that window, you move into survival strategies. For some people, that looks like too much activation, fight or flight energy, urgency, intensity, the need to fix or defend. For others, it looks like too little, freeze, shutdown, blankness, the sense that you've disappeared inside your own body. Either way, your options narrow, and it becomes much harder to do the wise, steady thing you *want* to do.

The long game of calm is not about avoiding discomfort forever. It's about widening that window so more of life can happen without your system tipping straight into protection mode. And the way you widen it is the same way you build any capacity in the body: You practice near the edge, you return, repair, and repeat.

That's why repetition matters more than intensity. A nervous system doesn't learn trust through heroic moments but through many small experiences of "I got activated . . . and I came back."

PART 2: HOW TRUST IS BUILT
THE DAILY EVIDENCE THAT CHANGES YOUR BASELINE

Trust doesn't arrive as a feeling. It arrives as a pattern.

It's the quiet shift that happens when your nervous system starts to expect that you will respond to rising stress with support, not abandonment. Over time, that expectation changes everything. Your system doesn't have to escalate as quickly because it no longer needs to shout to be heard.

In the background, your nervous system is always running a simple audit: When things get hard, do we get care or do we get criticized? When we're tired, do we rest or do we push until something breaks? When we make a mistake, do we repair or do we punish ourselves? When we're activated, do we slow down or speed up and make it worse?

You don't have to answer those questions perfectly. You just have to start answering them differently often enough that your body begins to believe you.

You stop using crisis as your rest strategy.

A lot of people only rest after they collapse. They do it because they're capable. They've learned to push through, to keep functioning, to keep carrying things. And when you live like that for long enough, rest starts to feel like something you earn, not something you need. The nervous system adapts to the expectation that relief will come later, after the work is done, after everyone else is okay, after the pressure drops.

The problem is that "later" is not a reliable plan, so the body takes matters into its own hands. It escalates. It forces a shutdown. It makes you sick, snappy, flat, flooded, or foggy. It's not trying to ruin your life, but it is trying to end the strain.

When you begin resting earlier, before you crash, or snap, or go numb, you change the whole contract. You teach your nervous system that it doesn't need to create a crisis to get your attention. That might look boring from the outside: eating before you're depleted, stepping outside for two minutes, going to bed instead of scrolling, taking a short reset rather than pushing through the last hour on fumes.

Boring is good. Boring is safe. Boring is where baseline gets built.

You respond to early signals instead of overriding them.

Most people can feel activation rising, but they don't act until it's too late.

They notice the jaw tension and keep talking. They notice the shallow breath and keep working. They notice the irritability and decide to "be better," which usually means more forcing. They notice the racing thoughts and keep trying to solve the whole problem at once.

That's overriding, and that teaches the nervous system a very specific lesson: Early signals don't lead to support. If early signals don't lead to support, the body learns it has to escalate. It has to get louder, stronger, more urgent, more intense because that's the only level that gets attention.

So, one of the most trust-building moves you can make is also one of the simplest. When you notice a signal, you respond. Not with drama, and not with perfection. Just with something small that brings your system down one notch.

You soften one place where you're bracing. You lengthen an exhale. You slow your pace. You pause before you respond. You choose the minimum effective action that reduces the climb. Over time, those small responses teach your nervous system that it can send a small signal and still be met.

You change your inner tone when you're activated.

People often treat self-talk like it's just "mindset." But your nervous system listens to how you interpret what's happening.

If every activation becomes a story of failure, such as *What's wrong with me? I'm doing it again. I should be past this,* the body hears threat on top of threat. Shame doesn't settle the nervous system; it escalates it. It adds pressure, urgency, and self-attack at the exact moment your system needs steadiness.

The shift here isn't fake positivity. It's accuracy with kindness and learning to meet activation with language that reduces threat instead of increasing it.

You might say to yourself, quietly, something like, "This is a nervous system event. It will pass," or you might remind your body, "Nothing has gone wrong," or you might offer a simple cue: "I can take one small step right now."

Those phrases aren't motivational posters. They're safety signals. And when those signals become familiar, your nervous system starts to trust that you won't turn stress into a moral trial.

You repair instead of replay.

When you get it wrong, because you will, what matters most is what happens next.

Some people replay. They rehearse the moment for hours, and they build a case against themselves. They punish themselves internally in the hope that punishment will prevent future mistakes. It doesn't. It usually just keeps the nervous system activated and teaches it that errors are dangerous.

Repair teaches a different lesson. Repair tells your system that rupture doesn't equal catastrophe, and that a hard moment can end in return instead of shame.

Repair can be internal. You notice you snapped, and instead of spiraling, you reset. You breathe, slow down, and choose your next move. You don't excuse the behavior, but you also don't attack yourself for being human.

Repair can also be relational. A clean apology. A restart. A simple ownership statement without a long defense. Those repairs build safety in relationships, but they also build safety in you. They teach your nervous system that you can come back, and that coming back is safe.

You become consistent with your boundaries.

Vague boundaries create constant scanning.

Should I say yes or no? How much can I take? How bad will it be if they're disappointed? How do I avoid conflict? When will this end?

That inner negotiation is exhausting, and exhaustion lowers your buffer. When your boundaries are unclear, your nervous system stays on alert because it doesn't know when protection is coming.

Consistent boundaries change that. Not harsh ones. Consistent ones. The kind where your body knows what happens next: If something escalates, you pause; if you're overloaded, you say no; if a conversation becomes unsafe, you step back and return when steadier.

Consistency is regulating because it reduces uncertainty. Your nervous system relaxes when it knows you won't keep abandoning yourself to keep the peace.

You practice stretch and return, not push and prove.

This is where a lot of people accidentally create the opposite of calm.

They try to build capacity by forcing themselves through overwhelm. They believe that if they just tolerate more, they'll become stronger. But overwhelm rarely builds trust. Overwhelm usually teaches the nervous system *See? It was too much.*

Capacity builds through stretch and return. You touch the edge of discomfort and stay connected enough to come back. You do the hard conversation, but you pause when you feel yourself tipping.

You do the challenging task, but you take breaks before you crash. You stay with emotion, but you keep yourself within range.

This is how the window widens—through repetition, not intensity. The nervous system learns *We can go there, and we can return.*

What Starts to Change

At first, these shifts don't look impressive. They're small and ordinary, and they often happen privately. But they compound.

You start noticing earlier because you've become more attuned. You spend less time in Red because you respond in Yellow. You recover faster after hard moments because you repair instead of punishing. You feel more like yourself more often because your nervous system is no longer treating everyday stress as a five-alarm fire.

That's what trust looks like in the body. Not the absence of activation, but the expectation of return.

Part 3: The Practice That Makes This Stick How to Develop Calm Without Turning It into Another Job

There's a moment in this work where people accidentally make calm feel like a performance.

They start monitoring themselves. They start collecting tools. They start aiming for the perfect regulated response. They treat every hard day as evidence that they're not progressing, and every slip as proof they've "gone backward."

It's understandable. Most of us were trained to improve through pressure. If you want change, you push. If you want results, you try harder. If you want to be better, you judge yourself into behaving differently.

But the nervous system doesn't learn through pressure the way the mind does. Pressure might produce short-term compliance, but it rarely produces long-term trust. Trust is built through steadiness. Through repetition. Through a relationship that feels safe enough to keep showing up.

So the practice that makes calm stick is not a bigger effort. It's a different relationship to effort.

It's learning how to practice in a way your nervous system can actually absorb.

What matters most is not the tool. It's the timing.

Most people use their tools when they're already in Red.

They reach for regulation when they're flooded, shut down, mid-argument, mid-spiral. And sometimes the tools still help, but the effort feels heavy because they're trying to steer a speeding car by tapping the brake.

The deeper shift happens when you start practicing in Yellow. Practicing earlier teaches your nervous system a new default. It learns that stress doesn't have to become a crisis before it gets support. It learns that the first sign of activation is a cue for care, not a cue for pushing through.

This is what makes calm feel more automatic over time. The pathway gets rehearsed when it's available, so it's easier to access when it's not.

The goal is a rhythm, not a routine.

A routine sounds like something you do perfectly or you fail.

A rhythm is something you return to.

That's much more aligned with how nervous systems actually change. You don't need a flawless morning ritual and an hour of meditation. You need a few reliable moments of return woven through the day, in ways that fit your real life.

A rhythm might include a small reset before you open your inbox. A pause before you walk into your house. A breath before you respond to a message. A short walk between tasks. A meal before you hit depletion. A boundary before resentment builds. A clean repair when you get it wrong.

None of those things is dramatic, but they're repetitive. And repetition is what your nervous system trusts.

Practice is "returning," not "getting it right."

This is one of the most important reframes in the whole book.

Progress is not measured by how often you get activated.

Progress is measured by how you respond to activation.

Do you spiral into shame, or do you return?

Do you punish yourself for being human, or do you support yourself back into range?

Do you treat a hard moment as proof you're broken or as a moment to practice a new response?

A nervous system learns trust through return. The return is the rep. The rep is the training.

If you think about it as building strength, it becomes easier to be kind to yourself. You don't walk into a gym, lift once, and decide you're weak forever. You lift, you rest, you repeat. You get a little stronger through consistent practice near your edge.

Calm works the same way. You don't become calm by never getting pulled. You become calm by practicing the pathway back.

Focus on three kinds of evidence.

When people get overwhelmed by this work, it's often because they're trying to change everything at once. They're attempting to fix sleep, food, exercise, boundaries, trauma, relationships, work stress, and their entire personality before Tuesday.

So instead, it helps to focus on three kinds of evidence, three categories of practice that build trust without turning calm into a second job.

The first is **evidence of care**.

These are the small moments where you show your nervous system "I'm paying attention." You eat. You rest. You slow down. You reduce stimulation. You lower the stakes. You choose something supportive instead of something punishing.

The second is **evidence of protection**.

These are the moments where you create safety through boundaries. You say no. You pause. You stop negotiating after you've been clear. You step away from escalation. You protect your time and energy before you hit resentment.

The third is **evidence of repair**.

These are the moments where you come back after rupture. You apologize cleanly. You reset. You restart the conversation. You stop replaying and start repairing. You return to yourself instead of abandoning yourself.

If you build those three categories of evidence consistently, your nervous system starts to change its expectations. It starts to believe you.

Don't chase calm. Chase capacity.

This is subtle, but it will save you a lot of frustration.

If you chase calm as a feeling, you'll keep measuring yourself against an ideal state that real life doesn't always allow. You'll interpret stress as failure. You'll treat activation as something to get rid of. And ironically, that makes activation worse, because the nervous system starts treating your own feelings as a threat.

If you chase capacity instead, everything gets easier.

Capacity is your ability to stay connected while life happens. Capacity is the ability to feel discomfort without being hijacked by it. Capacity is the ability to pause, choose, repair, and return.

And capacity grows through small, repeated returns to range, not through perfection.

So if you want a simple way to practice, try this question:

"What's the smallest thing I can do right now that helps my body stand down a notch?"

That question is gentle enough that your nervous system won't resist it. It's practical enough that you can answer it in the middle of real life. And it keeps the focus where it belongs: not on getting it right, but on returning.

The long game is quiet, and it works.

At some point, if you keep practicing like this, you'll notice something.

You'll still have hard days, but they won't take you down as far. You'll still get activated, but you'll come back sooner. You'll still feel triggered, but you'll be less scared of it. You'll still make mistakes, but you won't spiral as long.

That's calm becoming embodied because your nervous system has started to trust you. It knows you'll come back. It knows you won't abandon it. It knows that stress doesn't have to become a crisis before it gets support. And that trust becomes your baseline and the quiet foundation underneath everything else.

Part 4: What This Looks like in a Real-Life Week

Calm as a Skill, Not a Personality Trait

In the middle of a normal week, most people aren't failing because they don't have tools. They're failing because life doesn't arrive in neat conditions.

Calm gets tested when you're already behind. When your sleep is patchy. When someone is in a mood. When your inbox is relentless. When you're holding too many invisible things. When your baseline is already elevated, and the smallest spark suddenly feels like a fire.

So rather than imagining calm as a "state" you should live in, it helps to see it as a way of moving through your actual week. Not perfectly. Not spiritually. Just skillfully, with fewer unnecessary spirals and faster returns.

What follows isn't a routine. It's a picture of how trust gets built in real time with the kinds of moments where the nervous system learns *she's coming back for me*, even when the week is messy.

Monday: The Week Starts Before You Do

For many people, activation begins before the day has properly started. You wake up, and your mind is already running a list. Your body is already braced. You haven't even stood up yet, and you're negotiating with time.

In that moment, the trust-building move is not to "be calm." It's to stop adding pressure. It's to resist the urge to start the day by chasing the day.

Sometimes it looks like giving yourself thirty seconds before you pick up your phone. Sometimes it looks like eating something before coffee becomes a personality trait. Sometimes it looks like choosing one stabilizing action before you launch into output.

The point isn't the action itself. The point is the message: *We start with support.*

When you repeat that message, the nervous system learns it doesn't have to begin the week in fight-or-flight.

Midweek: The Invisible Load Starts to Show

By the middle of the week, most people have started overriding themselves.

They push through fatigue because they're "almost done." They keep saying yes because it feels easier than disappointing someone. They keep running on adrenaline because slowing down would mean feeling how tired they actually are.

This is where trust is either built or broken because your nervous system is watching what you do when you're overloaded. Does it get care, or does it get ignored? Do you respond to early signals, or do you force yourself through until you snap?

In a real week, this might look like pausing before replying to a message that spikes you. It might look like saying, "I can't do that today," without a ten-minute justification. It might look like stepping outside for two minutes between tasks so your body can downshift. It might look like choosing a minimum effective boundary with someone who tends to push.

None of it is dramatic. But it's evidence. And evidence is what changes baseline.

The Hard Conversation That Arrives at the Wrong Time

This is where calm becomes unmistakably practical.

The moment someone says something sharp. The moment a partner looks disappointed. The moment a colleague's tone lands wrong. The moment you feel the story in your head start to build, fast.

A nervous system that doesn't trust you will often do one of two things here. It will either over-function (explain, manage, smooth, fix, apologize, keep talking), or it will protect through shutdown or aggression. It will disappear, or it will fight.

So, the trust-building practice, in that moment, is not a perfect sentence. It's staying within range long enough to choose a safer move.

Sometimes the safer move is a pause. You buy time before you speak while you're flooded. You let your body come down one notch, so your words don't come out sharp or desperate.

Sometimes the safer move is one clean boundary. "I want to talk about this, but I'm not okay to do it in this tone," or "I need a minute before I respond," or "I can come back to this after dinner."

Sometimes the safer move is simply slowing down the pace. Fewer words. Lower volume. Longer exhale.

Those choices might feel small, but they are exactly how your nervous system learns a new outcome: *We can handle conflict without catastrophe. We can hold a line without going to war. We can stay connected without abandoning ourselves.*

THE MOMENT YOU GET IT WRONG

It's coming. It always does.

You snap at someone you love. You send the message too quickly. You go quiet. You over-explain. You react from the old program and realize it afterward.

This is where most people undo all their progress with shame. They treat the mistake as evidence that they're not changing, and then they punish themselves for it. The nervous system learns *Even when I'm struggling, I'm on my own.*

But there's a different pathway. The repair pathway.

When you repair, cleanly, calmly, without a performance, you teach your nervous system the opposite lesson. You teach it that mistakes aren't dangerous because return is available.

Sometimes repair is relational: "That came out sharper than I meant. I'm sorry. Let me try again." Sometimes repair is internal: "I'm activated. I'm not going to make this into a shame spiral. I'm going to reset and choose what happens next."

This is how trust gets built after a rupture. Not by never rupturing but by reliably returning.

THE WEEKEND: WHERE YOUR NERVOUS SYSTEM TELLS THE TRUTH

Weekends have a way of revealing what a nervous system has been carrying.

For some people, the weekend is relief. For others, it's when everything catches up. The body crashes, emotions appear, patience disappears, and it feels confusing because "nothing is happening."

But something has been happening. Your system has been running.

This is where the long game matters because the goal isn't just to cope better in emergencies. The goal is to live in a way that your nervous system doesn't need to scream for relief.

In a real-life week, trust-building might look like saying no to the extra thing even though you could technically squeeze it in. It might look like planning one restorative block instead of using the weekend to "catch up" on being a person. It might look like lowering stimulation, eating properly, moving your body, sleeping, and letting that be enough.

That will make your baseline easier to hold.

The Point of the Whole Week

When you zoom out, the practice is not about doing more. It's about becoming more reliable to yourself.

You show your nervous system, in dozens of small ways, that you will respond when it signals. You will protect what matters. You will repair when you get it wrong. You will rest before collapse. You will set boundaries before resentment. You will pause before you escalate. You will come back.

And over time, the nervous system stops treating life like a constant emergency because you are no longer treating *your own needs* like an inconvenience.

This is what calm starts to look like when it becomes embodied. Not a constant state. Not a personality trait. A relationship where your body learns, through lived evidence, that it can trust you.

PART 5: THE SETBACK PLAN
WHAT TO DO WHEN YOU FALL OFF THE WAGON
WITHOUT MAKING IT MEAN ANYTHING

At some point in this work, something will happen that makes you feel as if you've "lost it."

A week when sleep disappears. A stretch when you're overloaded. A conflict that gets under your skin. A few days when you're more reactive than you want to be. A period when you stop doing the things that help, and you can feel the baseline slipping.

This is not a sign that calm isn't real. It's a sign that you're human.

The mistake people make in these moments is not the setback itself. The mistake is the story they build about it. They treat a hard week like a character flaw. They interpret it as failure. They decide they've undone their progress, and then they punish themselves for it, which quietly keeps the nervous system activated for longer.

So this part is about something very practical: how to recover quickly, without drama, and without shame. Because if you want a nervous system that trusts you, you don't build that trust by never struggling. You build it by what you do when you *do* struggle. You build it by becoming reliable in the return.

Setbacks usually happen for three predictable reasons.

It helps to name this because it takes some of the mystery out of it.

Most setbacks are not psychological puzzles. They are predictable physiological outcomes.

The first is **baseline depletion**. You're tired, underfed, overstimulated, or carrying too much for too long. Your buffer shrinks, and things that normally wouldn't hook you start to land harder.

The second is **relational strain**. When connection feels shaky, the nervous system escalates quickly. A difficult conversation, conflict, rejection, criticism, disappointment are all strong cues for older patterns.

The third is **stacking stress**. Not one big dramatic event but a thousand small demands with no space between them. Your system never fully returns to neutral, so it starts living in Yellow, and it doesn't take much to tip into Red.

You don't need to analyze these reasons every time. You just need to recognize them so you don't treat the setback as personal failure. Often, it's just biology doing what biology does.

The rule that changes everything: Reset in 24 hours.

If you want a simple, forgiving plan, it's this:

Don't let a hard day become a hard week.

Don't force yourself into a perfect routine the next morning; just do a reset within a day. That reset can be small. It doesn't need to look impressive. It just needs to be real.

The reason this matters is not moral. It's learning.

Your nervous system is always learning what happens after stress. If stress is followed by shame, the system learns that stress is dangerous. If stress is followed by support, the system learns that stress is survivable.

So the quickest way to keep progress intact is not to avoid struggle. It's to shorten the gap between "I'm off track" and "I'm back."

THE MINIMUM EFFECTIVE RESET

When people hear "reset," they often imagine a full lifestyle overhaul.

They picture doing a huge workout, cooking clean meals, meditating for an hour, deleting social media, and becoming a different person by Tuesday.

That's the CEO trying to solve biology with ambition.

A nervous system responds better to something simpler: the minimum effective reset.

The minimum effective reset is the smallest set of actions that reliably brings your system down one notch and restores a bit of buffer. It's not about fixing your life. It's about getting you back within range.

In most cases, it involves three things: **body, environment, and one choice.**

You do something basic for the body. You eat. You hydrate. You sleep earlier if you can. You move your body gently. You reduce stimulation. You get outside. You let your physiology settle.

You do something basic for your environment. You lower the noise. You step away from what's escalating you. You create a little more space, even if it's only ten minutes.

Then you make one aligned choice. One thing that says, "I'm back on my own side." That might be cancelling something nonessential. It might be sending one clear boundary message instead of over-explaining. It might be taking a break before you keep going. It might be doing a clean repair instead of stewing.

The point is not the specific action. The point is the signal. Your nervous system receives it as evidence: *Support is available.*

What to Do When You're Tempted to Shame Yourself

Setbacks often trigger an old voice.

The voice that says you're lazy. Too sensitive. Not disciplined. Not consistent. The voice that tries to motivate you by making you feel bad.

If that voice has been running your life for a long time, it will show up here because shame is a familiar strategy for control. It believes that if you punish yourself hard enough, you won't repeat the mistake.

But shame doesn't build trust. It builds fear. So when you notice shame starting to spool up, it can help to treat it the way you would treat any other activation. Not as truth, but as a state shift that needs support. You don't have to argue with the shame voice. You can simply take your attention back to the reset. Back to the body. Back to the next small choice.

A helpful inner line is "This is a nervous system dip. The return is the work."

Because it is.

How You Know Your Progress Is Real

Here's the thing people often miss.

If you've done this work for a while, you may still have days where you react strongly, shut down, snap, spiral, or feel like you've lost your footing. The difference is what happens next.

Progress looks like noticing sooner and recovering faster, repairing instead of replaying, and less self-attack on the way back.

Progress looks like your nervous system trusting that return is possible because it has evidence that you return.

A setback is not the end of your progress. It's one of the places your progress gets built. Because every time you come back calmly, without drama, your nervous system learns the most important lesson of all: *We can handle this.*

And over time, that lesson becomes baseline.

Part 6: The Identity Shift
When Calm Stops Being Something You Practice and Starts Being How You Live

There's a moment that comes quietly in this work. It doesn't arrive with fireworks. It often doesn't even feel like a "moment" at the time.

You simply realize, one day, that you handled something differently.

Not perfectly, but differently. You felt the surge, and you didn't follow it all the way up. You paused before you replied. You set a boundary without a lecture. You noticed your own depletion before you became a version of yourself you don't like. You repaired cleanly instead of spiraling. You came back faster than you used to.

And the most surprising part is that you didn't do it because you remembered a strategy. You did it because it was becoming normal.

That's the identity shift.

It's not that you become calm as a personality trait. It's that you become someone your nervous system expects to be safe with. You become reliable. Not rigid, not perfect, not always regulated, just reliable.

This matters because the goal of this book isn't to give you a set of tools you must keep gripping tightly forever. The deeper goal is to help you build a baseline where those tools become less necessary because your system has learned a different default.

When calm becomes embodied, you still get activated, but the activation doesn't feel like a crisis. It feels like weather. Something that moves through. Something you can work with. It's a process you can guide.

What changes when identity shifts.

Early in this work, calm often feels like effort. You must remember to pause. You need to catch yourself mid-pattern and talk yourself into doing the supportive thing. You need to use the CEO to manage the Caveman, and some days it feels like running a daycare center with no staff.

As trust builds, that effort changes shape. You still have to practice, but you're no longer constantly negotiating with yourself. The supportive move becomes easier to access because your nervous system has more evidence that the supportive move works.

You start defaulting to the path of return.

You notice sooner because your system isn't as committed to ignoring early signals. You choose earlier because you're not waiting until you're flooded to take yourself seriously. You repair more cleanly because shame is no longer the only response you know. You feel more capacity for relationships because you're not constantly bracing for conflict or scanning for danger. You can tolerate discomfort without immediately turning it into urgency.

Even the way you interpret yourself changes. Instead of "I'm a reactive person," you start thinking, "My system gets activated sometimes, and I know how to come back." Instead of "I can't handle stress," it becomes "Stress affects me, and I have a pathway through it." The story is gentler, but it's also more accurate.

Calm becomes a form of self-respect.

This is one of the quieter truths underneath everything we've been building.

Calm, in the embodied sense, is not about becoming softer or nicer or more pleasant. It's not about smoothing over conflict. It's not about being endlessly patient. It's not about never getting angry or never needing anything.

It's about self-respect at the level of the nervous system.

It's the moment you stop abandoning yourself to keep the peace. The moment you stop overriding your body to meet a deadline. The moment you stop using self-attack as motivation. The moment you start treating your needs as real, your limits as valid, and your recovery as non-negotiable.

When you live that way repeatedly, your nervous system begins to relax because it no longer has to protect you from you.

That might sound strange, but it's often the truth. Many of us have spent years forcing ourselves, criticizing ourselves, and pushing through signals that were trying to help us. A nervous system that has been ignored will escalate. A nervous system that has been punished will brace. A nervous system that has been abandoned internally will look for safety through control.

So when you become the person who responds instead of overrides, protects instead of pleases, repairs instead of shames, the body starts to trust that it doesn't need to stay on high alert.

Your patterns don't disappear. They become less in charge.

The identity shift isn't the disappearance of old patterns. It's the reduction of their authority.

You might still have the urge to over-explain, but you can feel it and choose not to. You might still want to shut down in conflict, but you can name it and take a clean pause instead. You might still feel the pull of people-pleasing, but you can hold the discomfort of someone else's disappointment without abandoning yourself.

This is what real change looks like. Not becoming a different human but becoming a human with more choice.

Over time, the nervous system learns that it can tolerate more without tipping into protection mode because it trusts your ability to respond. The CEO has more influence because the Caveman isn't running the whole show.

The deepest marker of calm is your ability to return.

If you wanted one measure of progress that you could trust, it's this: how quickly and kindly you return.

Return is what builds baseline and changes your identity. It is what makes calm real.

You will still have days where you snap or shut down or spiral. The long game isn't to eliminate that. The long game is to shorten the distance between activation and support, between rupture and repair, between stress and return.

And the more often you return without shame, the more your nervous system starts to expect that return is available. It stops escalating to get your attention because it trusts you to notice sooner.

That's not just a skill. That's a relationship. And when that relationship is strong, calm stops being something you chase. It becomes something you live from.

Closing: Calm Is the Relationship You Build with Yourself

If you take one thing from this chapter, let it be this: Calm is not something you achieve once and then keep forever.

It's something you build.

You build it the same way you build trust with another person. You show up consistently. You respond when it matters. You repair when you get it wrong. You stop making your needs inconvenient. You become someone your nervous system can rely on.

That is what changes baseline.

Not willpower. Not perfect routines. Not forcing yourself to stay composed. The nervous system doesn't update because you *want* it to. It updates when it has enough lived evidence that it's safe to stand down. Evidence that you will pause before you escalate; rest before you collapse; hold a boundary before resentment builds; return without turning the moment into a shame trial.

And yes, life will still be life.

There will still be hard weeks. There will still be triggers. There will still be people who don't communicate well, deadlines that stretch you, moments where you surprise yourself in ways you don't love. The goal isn't to eliminate stress. The goal is to become less afraid of it because you trust your ability to meet it.

That's the identity shift. Not "I am calm all the time," but "When I'm not, I know how to come back."

When your nervous system trusts you, it doesn't need to shout as loudly, mobilize as early, or treat every discomfort like danger. It learns that the first sign of activation will be met, not ignored. That relief is available without a crisis. That you can feel a lot and still have choices.

And that's what calm really is. Not the absence of activation, but the expectation of return.

In the next chapter, we'll look at the final piece that makes all of this easier to sustain: how to design your life so your nervous system isn't constantly fighting uphill. Skills matter, but so does your environment. Calm isn't just something you practice in the moment. It's something you build into the way you live.

Chapter 11

CALM AS A WAY OF LIVING

Integration, Self-Leadership, and What Happens Next

At some point, calm stops being something you reach for when you're already drowning. It becomes the way you hold your life.

Not because nothing ever rattles you again, and not because you've turned into a serene woodland creature who glides through chaos while everyone else panics. Calm becomes real when your nervous system starts to trust the person living inside it. When you keep showing up as someone who returns, repairs, and protects what matters.

That's what this book has been building toward.

We started with a simple truth: Calm isn't a personality trait. It's a skill. A biological skill. Something you can develop, even if you've spent years feeling like your reactions are faster than your intentions.

Along the way, you learned to notice state, not just story. You learned why thinking tools don't work when your system is in protection mode. You learned how real-time regulation gives you back choice, and how triggers aren't proof that you're broken but information about what your nervous system has learned. You learned how boundaries and repair aren't just communication tools but safety signals that shape relationships from the inside out. You learned that calm becomes embodied through repetition, not perfection.

Now we get to do the final, quietly powerful thing: put it all together.

When calm is integrated, it doesn't stay in the "self-help" corner of your life. It changes how you parent, how you work, how you argue, how you make decisions, how you recover, how you speak to yourself, how you move through uncertainty. It becomes the foundation underneath everything else.

This chapter is the moment the whole thing clicks into a new worldview: **Calm isn't just something you experience. It's something you create.**

Not by controlling the world around you but by leading the one inside you.

Part 1: Self-Leadership Is Nervous System Leadership Living from Connection Mode

Most people think of leadership as something you do with other people. But the most important leadership in your life is the kind you practice internally, in private, when nobody is watching.

It's the leadership you bring to your own stress response.

When your nervous system is activated, do you abandon yourself and push through until you snap? Do you criticize yourself for having feelings? Do you override the early signals and then act surprised when you hit Red? Do you treat activation like an emergency or like weather?

This is where "self-leadership" stops being a motivational idea and becomes a biological skill. It's the ability to stay in relationship with yourself when your system is activated so your patterns don't run the whole show.

In earlier chapters, we talked about the CEO and the Caveman brain. You've already seen how the Caveman moves faster than your best intentions, and how the CEO can lose access under stress. The goal was never to fire the Caveman. The goal was to stop letting the Caveman run the company unsupervised.

Self-leadership is what keeps the CEO in the building.

Not through force, but through connection.

When you're in connection mode, you can still feel pressure and urgency, but you don't lose yourself. You can tolerate discomfort without turning it into catastrophe. Connection mode doesn't mean you're calm all the time. It means you stay reachable. You remain someone who can respond.

Protection mode is different. It prepares for impact. In protection mode, you might resort to fight, flight, freeze, or fawn. The strategy changes, but the goal is the same: reduce threat, preserve safety.

None of this makes you flawed. It makes you human.

The shift you've been practicing is the ability to recognize protection mode sooner and choose what happens next. That choice might be a breath, a pause, a boundary, a repair, a step away, a lowered stake, a minimum effective response. It might be as small as unclenching your jaw and slowing your voice by ten percent.

Small is not insignificant here. Small is how your nervous system learns.

Self-leadership isn't a grand declaration. It's a pattern of returns. And when you practice that pattern consistently, something changes in the background. Your nervous system begins to expect support instead of criticism, and it begins to trust that discomfort doesn't have to become a crisis to be taken seriously. It learns that connection is available, not just with other people, but with you.

That's the heart of living from connection mode: **You stay on your own side.**

Not in a self-absorbed way. In a grounded way. The kind of grounded that makes you easier to be around because you're not asking the world to regulate you while you abandon yourself internally. You become the steady reference point your own system can borrow from.

This is the internal shift that changes everything: You stop aiming for "I should be calm," and you start living as someone who knows how to create calm in your body, in your relationships, in your choices, and in the environments you build.

And once that's in place, the rest becomes much simpler. Not easy, but simpler. Life stops feeling like something that's happening *to* you and starts feeling like something you can meet with steadiness.

Part 2: Calm in the Places It Matters Most
Work, Parenting, Relationships, Health, and Decisions

When calm becomes integrated, it stops living in the category of "self-care."

It becomes the way you move through the parts of life that used to hook you the hardest. The goal isn't to become unbothered. The goal is to stay connected enough to choose how you respond, even when things are messy.

So, let's bring this down from theory into the places you actually live.

Calm at Work: Staying Steady in Systems That Speed You Up

Most modern work environments are not designed for nervous system health. They're designed for output, speed, responsiveness, and constant context-switching. Even when you love your job, the structure can quietly keep you in Yellow, always a little braced, a little behind, and a little "on."

Calm at work is rarely about feeling peaceful. It's about building micro-safety into your day so your system isn't running uphill the entire time.

That might look like creating a small buffer before you open your email so your nervous system doesn't start the day being yanked around by other people's urgency. It might look like pausing before you respond to a message that spikes you, so your reply comes from the CEO, not the Caveman. It might look like choosing fewer priorities because overload narrows your thinking and makes you less effective.

Calm at work also shows up in how you handle pressure. Some people cope by over-functioning. They take responsibility for everything, anticipate every problem, carry other people's emotions, and try to control outcomes so they don't get surprised. It looks competent, but it's exhausting, and it trains the nervous system to believe that safety requires vigilance.

A steadier form of calm is learning to be clear instead of reactive. You set expectations. You communicate limits early. You don't agree to timelines while you're flooded. You pause, check your capacity, and then respond. That one change, responding instead of reflexively complying, reduces the background load more than most people realize.

Calm in Parenting: Leading the Room with Your Nervous System

Parenting is a nervous system sport.

You can have all the knowledge in the world, but when a child is dysregulated, your system receives that as a cue. Your body reads urgency. Your attention narrows. Your voice tightens. Your patience shrinks.

And because children borrow nervous system cues, your internal state often matters more than your words.

Calm in parenting doesn't mean you never get frustrated. It means you practice returning to steadiness more quickly, and you stop interpreting dysregulation, yours or theirs, as moral failure.

Sometimes calm is lowering your shoulders while you're stating the boundary. Sometimes it's slowing your voice by ten percent.

Sometimes it's giving yourself permission to pause instead of escalating. Sometimes it's repairing after you've snapped, so your child learns the most important relational lesson: Hard moments can end in return.

This is one of the quiet gifts of embodied calm. You stop trying to parent perfectly, and you start modelling something more valuable: how to be human under stress and still come back.

Calm in Relationships: Less Reactivity, More Repair

When calm is integrated, relationships stop feeling like a constant negotiation between your needs and other people's comfort.

You become more able to hold your truth without turning it into a threat. More able to tolerate someone else's disappointment without abandoning yourself. More able to pause in conflict without making it mean disconnection. More willing to repair because you're no longer terrified of being "the problem."

This is where boundaries and calm are deeply linked. A nervous system that can't hold boundaries will often keep living in low-grade anxiety. It's constantly scanning for what people need, what might go wrong, what you should say, how to keep things stable. That scanning looks like care, but it's often fear.

As calm deepens, your relationships tend to become simpler. Not necessarily easier, but less chaotic internally. You can speak more directly. You can say no with fewer words. You can notice when the pattern is starting and take a relational reset before it becomes a blow-up.

And when something does rupture, you can repair cleanly instead of spiraling. Repair becomes a normal part of love, not an emergency procedure.

Calm in Your Health: The Baseline Your Body Lives In

Your body does not experience stress as an idea. It experiences stress as chemistry.

If your nervous system spends most days in Yellow, your body adapts to that. Sleep becomes lighter. Digestion can be affected. Muscles stay tense. Hormones shift. You might feel wired and tired at the same time, or flat and foggy, or constantly "on edge" without being able to point to one big reason.

This is why calm is not just a mindset practice. It's a health practice.

When you build a steadier baseline, your body often starts to cooperate in ways that surprise you. Your sleep improves. Your appetite cues become clearer. Your energy becomes less volatile. Your recovery gets better. You feel more resilient because your system isn't constantly burning fuel just to stay functional.

This isn't about chasing perfect wellbeing. It's about reducing unnecessary stress load so your body isn't fighting uphill all the time.

Calm in Decision-Making: Choosing from Values, Not Chemistry

One of the most practical results of embodied calm is that your decisions improve.

When you're activated, you tend to decide from urgency. You say yes too quickly. You send the message too fast. You make the purchase. You quit the thing. You react to discomfort as if it's an instruction.

When you're steadier, you can feel discomfort without needing to resolve it immediately. You can hold uncertainty without making a panicked decision just to end the feeling. You can pause long enough to ask, "What do I actually want here?" and "What aligns with my values?" rather than "What will make this sensation go away right now?"

That pause is the CEO returning.

It's also why calm is a leadership skill, not just a personal wellness goal. Calm increases the space between stimulus and response, and that space is where better choices live.

The Thread That Ties It All Together

In each of these areas (work, parenting, relationships, health, decisions), the shift is not that you never get activated.

The shift is that you stop letting activation run the whole day.

You learn to recognize what state you're in and respond accordingly. You practice lowering the baseline, so you have more buffer. You hold boundaries earlier. You repair sooner. You come back without shame.

This is what it means for calm to become a way of living. It's not a special state you visit occasionally. It's the foundation you build under ordinary life, so ordinary life doesn't feel like a constant threat.

And when that foundation is strong, the work becomes less about fixing yourself and more about designing your life to support the version of you that's already emerging.

PART 3: DESIGNING A LIFE THAT MAKES CALM EASIER

THE ENVIRONMENTS YOUR NERVOUS SYSTEM LEARNS FROM

By now, it should be clear that calm isn't just something you do in a moment.

It's something you build into the way you live.

This matters because a lot of people approach nervous system work like a character project. They assume the entire burden is internal: "I should be better at regulating." "I should be more resilient." "I should be able to handle more."

But your nervous system isn't only shaped by your mindset. It's shaped by your environment, your pace, your inputs, the expectations you live under, and what you repeatedly ask your body to tolerate.

If your life is structured in a way that constantly pushes you into Yellow, then calm will always feel like something you're trying to hold against the current. You might get good at returning, and that matters, but you'll also keep asking your system to fight uphill.

So, part of integration is stepping back and asking a different kind of question.

Not "How do I stay calm in this life?"

But "How do I build a life that makes calm more likely?"

Your nervous system learns from what's normal, not what's ideal.

Most people have a picture of the life they *should* have. A tidy schedule. Enough time. A calm morning routine. Fewer demands. Healthier habits. Better boundaries. More space.

And then they have the life they actually have.

The mistake is trying to practice calm in a life that is fundamentally unlivable and assuming the nervous system is the problem. In reality, your nervous system is responding appropriately to the conditions it's in. If those conditions are chronically overstimulating or chronically demanding, it's not weakness that you feel braced. It's accuracy.

Designing a calm, supportive life doesn't mean quitting your job and moving to the mountains. It means looking honestly at what your nervous system is being asked to tolerate as "normal" and then adjusting where you can.

Not all at once. Not as a total overhaul. Just enough to shift the baseline.

Design is not control. It's reducing unnecessary load.

A calm life is not a life with no stress.

It's a life where stress isn't stacked needlessly.

Some stress is meaningful. Work that matters. Parenting. Relationships. Growth. Challenge. Those things are part of being alive. But there's also a kind of stress that comes from poor design: constant urgency, constant switching, constant noise, constant access, constant self-neglect disguised as productivity.

Your nervous system experiences all of that as load.

So, the design question becomes "Where is the load unnecessary?"

Where can you remove friction, reduce decisions, lower stimulation, or create buffer and build a baseline that can hold more?

Buffer is a nervous system strategy.

Most people schedule their lives as if transitions don't exist.

They go from one meeting to the next. One demand to the next. One conversation to the next. One screen to the next. Then they wonder why they feel edgy, impatient, flat, or reactive.

Transitions are where the nervous system catches up. Without them, your system never fully returns. It just accumulates activation.

So, one of the simplest design upgrades is buffer.

A small buffer before you open your inbox. A buffer between tasks. A buffer after hard conversations. A buffer before you walk in the door. A buffer before you respond to someone else's urgency.

Buffer doesn't have to be long. Often it's minutes. But it changes the nervous system's experience of the day. It creates small windows where your body can downshift, which makes it less likely to tip into protection mode later.

Reduce decisions where you can.

Decision fatigue is not a moral problem. It's a capacity problem.

Every decision draws on cognitive and emotional resources. When you're already carrying a lot, small decisions start to feel strangely hard. What should we have for dinner? When should I reply to that message? What should I wear? Do I have time to exercise? How do I fit everything in?

None of those decisions is huge, but when they pile up, your nervous system starts treating the day like a constant problem to solve.

This is why reducing decisions can be profoundly calming. It's not about being rigid. It's about removing unnecessary friction.

Protect your inputs!

If your nervous system is constantly scanning, then what you feed it matters.

Noise, notifications, endless news cycles, constant social comparison, aggressive work communication, too many open loops, these all keep the system in a low-grade alert state. Even when you're sitting still, your nervous system is processing threat cues.

A calm, supportive life often includes input boundaries as protection. You decide when you check your email. You decide when you consume information. You decide what you expose yourself to when you're already tired. You decide what conversations you're available for. You reduce the background buzz so your nervous system has more room.

This is one of the least glamorous and most powerful parts of calm.

Build anchors that bring you back to yourself.

A calm-supportive life has anchors.

Anchors are the small, reliable things that remind your body what "safe enough" feels like. They can be physical: movement, sunlight, water, meals, sleep. They can be relational: one person you feel steady with, one conversation that nourishes you rather than drains you. They can be structural: a weekly rhythm, a regular reset, a protected block of time.

Anchors don't need to be impressive. They need to be consistent because consistency is what your nervous system trusts.

The goal is not to optimize your life. It's to support your biology.

If you take this too far, calm becomes another performance. Another project. Another way to feel behind.

So, keep it simple.

You are not trying to build a perfect life. You're trying to build a life that doesn't constantly require your nervous system to override itself. You're trying to reduce unnecessary load, so you have more capacity for the parts of life that matter.

When you do that, calm stops being something you fight for. It becomes the natural result of how you live.

And this is one of the most empowering truths in the whole book: You don't have to force your nervous system into calm.

You can design your life so that calm has room to happen.

Part 4: The Calm Plan A Simple Way to Keep This Alive Without Turning It into a "Program"

By this point, you've read enough to know there's no single tool that solves everything.

There are moments when breath is enough, moments when you need movement, moments when you need a boundary, moments when you need repair, and moments when you simply need sleep and a sandwich. Calm is not a one-trick pony. It's a relationship with your nervous system that gets expressed in different ways, depending on what life is throwing at you.

So instead of giving you a complicated plan that you'll follow for a week and then abandon, I want to offer something simpler: a way of holding this work that fits inside real life.

Think of it as a calm plan, not a program. A set of principles you can return to. A few reliable questions that bring you back to work without turning it into another job.

Start with one daily anchor.

If you do nothing else, choose one small daily anchor that supports your baseline. Not a heroic routine. Not an identity overhaul. One thing that tells your nervous system, "We do care for ourselves here."

It might be a short walk, a protein-heavy breakfast, ten minutes of quiet before the house wakes up, sunlight on your face, going to bed earlier by half an hour, or a boundary around when you check email.

The point isn't which anchor you choose. The point is that it's consistent. Consistency is safety. When your nervous system can predict one supportive act every day, it stops living as if support only happens in emergencies.

Use a mid-day check-in that doesn't require overthinking.

A lot of people only realize they're dysregulated when they're already in Red. So, build a tiny check-in point into your day, something you can do without journaling, analyzing, or turning it into a performance.

You can ask yourself, "What gear am I in right now?" or "Am I within my window?" or simply, "Am I still reachable?"

If the answer is yes, the goal is not to become calmer. The goal is to stay within range. That usually means one small downshift: exhale, soften, slow, widen.

If the answer is no, the goal changes. You stop trying to fix the whole situation, and you move into containment. Fewer words. Less stimulation. Ground through the body. Create space. Come back to what helps your nervous system stand down.

This check-in is not about constant monitoring. It's about earlier support. Earlier support is what changes baseline.

Make one "minimum effective" boundary part of your life.

Most people burn out not because they never rest but because they don't have enough boundaries.

They keep absorbing other people's urgency. They keep saying yes when their body is saying no. They keep negotiating with themselves until they're resentful. They keep trying to be easy to deal with, and then they wonder why they feel brittle.

So, choose one boundary that would make your nervous system feel safer. Something small but structural. A line that reduces scanning. A decision that removes daily negotiation.

It might be a boundary around work hours; around how quickly you respond to messages; around what you will and won't discuss when you're tired; around your phone in the morning; around one relationship pattern you keep tolerating.

The reason this matters is not because boundaries are "healthy." It's because boundaries reduce uncertainty, and uncertainty is one of the nervous system's biggest triggers.

Schedule one reset per week.

If your week is full, your nervous system needs a predictable exhale. Not a vacation. Not a wellness retreat. A reset. A block of time where you are not producing, performing, or fixing. A block of time where your system is allowed to come back to neutral.

This might be a solo walk. A class. A nap. A long shower. A slow morning. Time in nature. A phone-free afternoon. A café with a notebook. It can be anything that actually feels like a downshift in your body.

The important part is that it's planned. When resets are only spontaneous, they tend to disappear. When they're built into the structure of your week, your nervous system starts to trust that relief is coming.

Treat repair as a normal skill, not a sign you failed.

One of the most powerful ways to make calm sustainable is to normalize repair.

You will still get activated. You will still say the wrong thing sometimes. You will still have moments where you overreact, withdraw, people-please, or go sharp. That's not a contradiction of progress. It's part of being a person with a nervous system.

Repair keeps those moments from turning into identity stories.

Instead of "I'm terrible," it becomes "I was activated, and I can come back."

Instead of "That relationship is ruined," it becomes "We had a rupture, and we can repair."

Instead of replaying for days, you reset and return.

When repair becomes normal, your nervous system relaxes because it stops treating mistakes as catastrophic. It learns that even hard moments can end in reconnection, and that changes everything.

The Calm Plan in One Question

If all of this feels like too much to hold, come back to one question:

"What's the smallest thing I can do right now that helps my nervous system feel safer?"

That question is gentle enough to work when you're overwhelmed. Practical enough to answer in real life. Flexible enough to apply in any situation.

The answer might be a pause, a boundary, food, breath, sleep, asking for help, or saying no. None of these is glamorous, but they are the work. They are the evidence that builds trust. And when you keep giving your nervous system that evidence, calm stops being something you chase. It becomes something your life supports.

Part 5: The Final Integration
What You Know Now, and What Changes Because of It

If you've made it this far, you've already learned something most people never get taught: Your stress response isn't a personality defect. It's a system doing what it was designed to do. The reason "just calm down" has never worked is not because you're stubborn or fragile, but because the nervous system doesn't change through intention alone. It changes through evidence.

That's the thread running through this entire book. You are not trying to become a different person. You are building a different relationship with your own biology, one that makes it easier to stay connected to yourself when life gets loud.

One of the most important shifts is that you stop trying to solve the wrong problem. When you're activated, you stop expecting yourself to be insightful and articulate while your system is in protection mode. You don't demand perspective from a brain that is temporarily prioritizing survival. You support the body first because once the body begins to settle, the mind becomes available again. This is why state comes before story and why real calm starts in the nervous system, not in your thoughts.

You also learn to reinterpret what used to feel like failure. Triggers stop being proof that you're broken and start becoming information about what your nervous system has learned. Overreactions stop being embarrassing mysteries and start becoming clues. You begin to recognize that some reactions are about what is happening now, and some are about what this moment resembles. That understanding doesn't magically erase the reaction, but it changes how you relate to it. It removes the shame layer, and shame is often the thing that keeps the reaction stuck.

The same is true in relationships. Instead of trying to win a conversation while you're flooded, you start prioritizing nervous system safety, yours and the other person's, because you've seen what happens when protection mode takes over. You learn how to pause without abandoning, how to set boundaries without going cold, and how to repair without groveling. The result is not a life with no conflict but a life with fewer spirals, shorter ruptures, and more return.

And then there's baseline, the quiet foundation underneath everything. You begin to see how much of what you thought was "emotional" was actually biological depletion: too little rest, too many decisions, too much stimulation, too much stacking stress, too many open loops. When baseline is low, everything hits harder. When baseline is steadier, you have more buffer. That buffer doesn't make life perfect, but it gives you more access to choice, and choice is the real point of calm.

Over time, the change becomes visible in a way that's almost strangely ordinary. You still get activated, but you notice earlier. You still have hard days, but you recover faster. You still have triggers, but you can hold them with more steadiness and less self-attack. You still make mistakes, but you repair rather than punish yourself. Setbacks stop turning into identity stories because you know how to return. Not perfectly, but reliably.

This is what it looks like when calm becomes a skill rather than a goal. You're no longer chasing a state you hope will arrive one day. You're building capacity in the body, safety in the relationships that matter, and trust in yourself. You're teaching your nervous system that discomfort doesn't have to become a crisis before it gets support, and that you don't have to abandon yourself to keep functioning.

A calmer life, in this sense, is not necessarily a quieter life. It's still a human life, with pressure and uncertainty and change. The difference is that you become less afraid of your own activation because you understand it and you have a pathway through it. You stop treating stress as proof that something is wrong with you, and you start treating it as a signal you can work with.

That's the integration. It isn't dramatic. It's deeply practical. It's the quiet moment, again and again, where you choose support over criticism, boundaries over resentment, repair over replay, and return over shame. Those choices become evidence. That evidence becomes trust. And trust becomes baseline.

Closing: The Last Page

If you're holding this book at the end, there's a good chance you've spent a long time trying to do life "the right way" while your nervous system was doing something else entirely. You've probably had times when you knew what to do in theory but couldn't access it in the moment. You've wondered why the same patterns keep showing up, even when you're smart, self-aware, and trying hard.

So let me leave you with the simplest truth I can offer.

Nothing has gone wrong.

Your nervous system has been doing its job, often with the best strategies it had available at the time. Some of those strategies might not fit your life anymore, but they made sense when they were learned. And the fact that you're here, learning, noticing, practicing return, is evidence that you are not stuck. You are already changing.

The work from here is not about becoming someone new. It's about becoming more at home in yourself. More importantly, it's about building trust.

Trust that you can feel a lot without being taken out by it. Trust that you can have hard conversations and still stay connected to yourself. Trust that you can make mistakes and come back. Trust that stress is something you can move through, not something that defines you.

That trust doesn't come from one big breakthrough. It comes from repetition.

A book can give you the map. It can help you name what's happening and why. It can give you language and frameworks and the first steps of return. But practice is where this becomes yours. Practice is where calm stops being an idea and starts becoming a way of living, in your work, your relationships, your parenting, your health, and your internal world.

So that's the invitation, as you close this.

Keep practicing return.

Not perfectly. Not relentlessly. Just consistently enough that your nervous system starts to believe you. Because calm is not the absence of activation. Calm is the ability to return, and you are already building that skill.

You don't have to do it all today.

Just come back, again and again, to the next small thing that helps your body feel safe enough to be here.

BIBLIOGRAPHY

Aldao, Amelia, Susan Nolen-Hoeksema, and Susanne Schweizer. "Emotion-Regulation Strategies across Psychopathology: A Meta-Analytic Review." *Clinical Psychology Review* 30, no. 2 (2010): 217–237. https://doi.org/10.1016/j.cpr.2009.11.004.

Arnsten, Amy F. T. "Stress Signalling Pathways That Impair Prefrontal Cortex Structure and Function." *Nature Reviews Neuroscience* 10, no. 6 (2009): 410–422. https://doi.org/10.1038/nrn2648.

Barrett, Lisa Feldman. "The Theory of Constructed Emotion: An Active Inference Account of Interoception and Categorization." *Social Cognitive and Affective Neuroscience* 12, no. 1 (2017): 1–23. https://doi.org/10.1093/scan/nsw154.

Baumeister, Roy F., Ellen Bratslavsky, Mark Muraven, and Dianne M. Tice. "Ego Depletion: Is the Active Self a Limited Resource?" *Journal of Personality and Social Psychology* 74, no. 5 (1998): 1252–1265. https://doi.org/10.1037/0022-3514.74.5.1252.

Bratman, Gregory N., J. Paul Hamilton, and Gretchen C. Daily. "The Impacts of Nature Experience on Human Cognitive

Function and Mental Health." *Annals of the New York Academy of Sciences* 1249, no. 1 (2012): 118–136. https://doi.org/10.1111/j.1749-6632.2011.06400.x.

Coan, James A., Hillary S. Schaefer, and Richard J. Davidson. "Lending a Hand: Social Regulation of the Neural Response to Threat." *Psychological Science* 17, no. 12 (2006): 1032–1039. https://doi.org/10.1111/j.1467-9280.2006.01832.x.

Craig, A. D. (Arthur D.). "How Do You Feel—Now? The Anterior Insula and Human Awareness." *Nature Reviews Neuroscience* 10, no. 1 (2009): 59–70. https://doi.org/10.1038/nrn2555.

Cramer, Holger, Romy Lauche, Jost Langhorst, and Gustav Dobos. "Yoga for Depression: A Systematic Review and Meta-Analysis." *Depression and Anxiety* 30, no. 11 (2013): 1068–1083. https://doi.org/10.1002/da.22166.

Critchley, Hugo D., and Sarah N. Garfinkel. "Interoception and Emotion." *Current Opinion in Psychology* 17 (2017): 7–14. https://doi.org/10.1016/j.copsyc.2017.04.020.

Eisenberger, Naomi I. "The Neural Bases of Social Pain: Evidence for Shared Representations with Physical Pain." *Psychosomatic Medicine* 74, no. 2 (2012): 126–135. https://doi.org/10.1097/PSY.0b013e3182464dd1.

Feldman, Ruth. "Mother-Infant Synchrony and the Development of Moral Orientation in Childhood and Adolescence: Direct and Indirect Mechanisms of Developmental Continuity." *American Journal of Orthopsychiatry* 77, no. 4 (2007): 582–597. https://doi.org/10.1037/0002-9432.77.4.582.

Gross, James J. "Emotion Regulation: Current Status and Future Prospects." *Psychological Inquiry* 26, no. 1 (2015): 1–26. https://doi.org/10.1080/1047840X.2014.940781.

Hagger, Martin S., Chantelle Wood, Chris Stiff, and Nikos L. D. Chatzisarantis. "Ego Depletion and the Strength Model of Self-Control: A Meta-Analysis." *Psychological Bulletin* 136, no. 4 (2010): 495–525. https://doi.org/10.1037/a0019486.

Holt-Lunstad, Julianne, Timothy B. Smith, Mark Baker, Tyler Harris, and David Stephenson. "Loneliness and Social Isolation as Risk Factors for Mortality: A Meta-Analytic Review." *Perspectives on Psychological Science* 10, no. 2 (2015): 227–237. https://doi.org/10.1177/1745691614568352.

Hopper, Susan I., Sarah L. Murray, Laura R. Ferrara, and Jennifer K. Singleton. "Effectiveness of Diaphragmatic Breathing for Reducing Physiological and Psychological Stress in Adults: A Quantitative Systematic Review." *JBI Database of Systematic Reviews and Implementation Reports* 17, no. 9 (2019): 1855–1876. https://doi.org/10.11124/JBISRIR-2017-003848.

Jerath, Ravinder, James W. Edry, Vernon A. Barnes, and Vandana Jerath. "Physiology of Long Pranayamic Breathing." *Medical Hypotheses* 67, no. 3 (2006): 566–571. https://doi.org/10.1016/j.mehy.2006.02.042.

Killgore, William D. S. "Effects of Sleep Deprivation on Cognition." *Progress in Brain Research* 185 (2010): 105–129. https://doi.org/10.1016/B978-0-444-53702-7.00007-5.

Kolacz, Jacek, Katja K. Kovacic, and Stephen W. Porges. "Traumatic Stress and the Autonomic Brain-Gut Connection in Development." *Developmental Psychobiology* 61, no. 5 (2019): 796–809. https://doi.org/10.1002/dev.21852.

Kredlow, M. Alexandra, Rebecca J. Fenster, Elizabeth S. Laurent, Kerry J. Ressler, and Elizabeth A. Phelps. "Prefrontal Cortex, Amygdala, and Threat Processing: Implications for PTSD." *Neuropsychopharmacology* 47, no. 1 (2022): 247–259. https://doi.org/10.1038/s41386-021-01155-7.

LeDoux, Joseph E. "Emotion Circuits in the Brain." *Annual Review of Neuroscience* 23 (2000): 155–184. https://doi.org/10.1146/annurev.neuro.23.1.155.

Lieberman, Matthew D., Naomi I. Eisenberger, Molly J. Crockett, Sabrina M. Tom, Jennifer H. Pfeifer, and Baldwin M. Way. "Putting Feelings into Words: Affect Labeling Disrupts Amygdala Activity." *Psychological Science* 18, no. 5 (2007): 421–428. https://doi.org/10.1111/j.1467-9280.2007.01916.x.

Lin, Xi, Jing Zheng, Qiang Zhang, and Yi Li. "The Effects of Mind-Body Exercise on Anxiety." *Mental Health and Physical Activity* 26 (2024): Article 100587. https://doi.org/10.1016/j.mhpa.2024.100587.

Mayer, John D., Peter Salovey, and David R. Caruso. "Emotional Intelligence: New Ability or Eclectic Traits?" *American Psychologist* 63, no. 6 (2008): 503–517. https://doi.org/10.1037/0003-066X.63.6.503.

McEwen, Bruce S. "Physiology and Neurobiology of Stress and Adaptation: Central Role of the Brain." *Physiological Reviews* 87, no. 3 (2007): 873–904. https://doi.org/10.1152/physrev.00041.2006.

Nolen-Hoeksema, Susan, Blair E. Wisco, and Sonja Lyubomirsky. "Rethinking Rumination." *Perspectives on Psychological Science* 3, no. 5 (2008): 400–424. https://doi.org/10.1111/j.1745-6924.2008.00088.x.

Palmer, Carol A., and Candice A. Alfano. "Sleep and Emotion Regulation: An Organizing, Integrative Review." *Sleep Medicine Reviews* 31 (2017): 6–16. https://doi.org/10.1016/j.smrv.2015.12.006.

Pascoe, Michaela C., and Ian E. Bauer. "A Systematic Review of Randomised Control Trials on the Effects of Yoga." *Journal of Psychiatric Research* 68 (2015): 270–282. https://doi.org/10.1016/j.jpsychires.2015.07.013.

Peña-Sarrionandia, Ander, Moïra Mikolajczak, and James J. Gross. "Integrating Emotion Regulation and Emotional Intelligence Traditions." *Frontiers in Psychology* 6 (2015): Article 160. https://doi.org/10.3389/fpsyg.2015.00160.

Pignatiello, Grant A., Richard J. Martin, and Ronald L. Hickman. "Decision Fatigue: A Conceptual Analysis." *Journal of Health Psychology* 25, no. 1 (2020): 123–135. https://doi.org/10.1177/1359105318763510.

Porges, Stephen W. "The Polyvagal Perspective." *Biological Psychology* 74, no. 2 (2007): 116–143. https://doi.org/10.1016/j.biopsycho.2006.06.009.

Porges, Stephen W. *The Polyvagal Theory: Neurophysiological Foundations of Emotions, Attachment, Communication, and Self-Regulation.* W. W. Norton & Company, 2011.

Porges, Stephen W. "Polyvagal Theory: A Science of Safety." *Frontiers in Integrative Neuroscience* 16 (2022): Article 871227. https://doi.org/10.3389/fnint.2022.871227.

Russell, George, and Stafford Lightman. "The Human Stress Response." *Nature Reviews Endocrinology* 15, no. 9 (2019): 525–534. https://doi.org/10.1038/s41574-019-0228-0.

Saghir, Zainab, J. N. Syeda, A. S. Muhammad, and T. H. B. Abdalla. "The Amygdala, Sleep Debt, Sleep Deprivation, and Anger." *Cureus* 10, no. 7 (2018): e2912. https://doi.org/10.7759/cureus.2912.

Salmon, Peter. "Effects of Physical Exercise on Anxiety, Depression, and Sensitivity to Stress." *Clinical Psychology Review* 21, no. 1 (2001): 33–61. https://doi.org/10.1016/S0272-7358(99)00032-X.

Sapolsky, Robert M. *Why Zebras Don't Get Ulcers.* 3rd ed. Holt Paperbacks, 2004.

Singh, B., Tim Olds, R. Curtis, et al. "Effectiveness of Physical Activity Interventions." *British Journal of Sports Medicine* 57, no. 18 (2023): 1203–1209. https://doi.org/10.1136/bjsports-2022-106195.

Tempesta, Daniela, Valentina Socci, Luigi De Gennaro, and Michele Ferrara. "Sleep and Emotional Processing." *Sleep Medicine Reviews* 40 (2018): 183–195. https://doi.org/10.1016/j.smrv.2017.12.005.

Torre, Jared B., and Matthew D. Lieberman. "Putting Feelings into Words: Affect Labeling as Implicit Emotion Regulation."

Emotion Review 10, no. 2 (2018): 116–124. https://doi.org/10.1177/1754073917742706.

White, Mathew P., Ian Alcock, Joanne Grellier, et al. "Spending at Least 120 Minutes a Week in Nature." *Scientific Reports* 9, no. 1 (2019): Article 7730. https://doi.org/10.1038/s41598-019-44097-3.

Zaccaro, Andrea, Andrea Piarulli, Maria Laurino, et al. "How Breath-Control Can Change Your Life." *Frontiers in Human Neuroscience* 12 (2018): Article 353. https://doi.org/10.3389/fnhum.2018.00353

ACKNOWLEDGMENTS

I want to thank the people I love most—the ones who, in different ways, helped shape not only this book, but me.

To Delta – thank you for the moment that sparked this entire idea. When you told your friends, so simply and so naturally, that "my mum doesn't do anger," you probably had no idea what those words would mean to me. But in that moment, something landed. You helped me see that calm is not just a private practice or a personal trait—it is something other people can feel in us. Something they remember. Something that changes the atmosphere around us. This book began with that moment, and with you.

To Wilson – thank you for the laughter. Thank you for your lightness, your humour, and your ability to pull me out of my own head and back into the moment. You have a way of moving through life that feels like a masterclass in low cortisol, and being around you is its own kind of medicine. Thank you for the joy you bring and for all the times you made life feel lighter.

To Marcus – thank you for teaching me what it means to be a parent. You made me grow in ways I never could have imagined, and you trusted me while I figured out so much of it on the run. Thank you for your love, your patience, and for surviving—and somehow still respecting—some truly questionable parenting choices. Loving you has been one of the greatest teaching moments of my life, and being your parent has shaped me more than words can say.

Finally, to Mike – thank you for being my rock, my safe harbor, and my calm place to land. Your love has been a steadying force in my life. In a world that can feel noisy and demanding, you have been peace. Thank you for believing in me, for cheering me on, for holding me up when I've needed it, and for reminding me, again and again, that strength does not always have to be loud. Sometimes it looks like kindness. Sometimes it looks like steadiness. Sometimes it looks like you.

This book may carry my name, but it was written in the presence of love. It was shaped by the people who made me laugh, made me stronger, trusted me, grounded me, and gave me somewhere soft to land. For all of that, and for all of you, I am deeply grateful.

ABOUT THE AUTHOR

Melinda Charlesworth has spent her life helping capable people stay steady under pressure. Her experience as a leadership facilitator, professional speaker, management consultant, and serial "I wonder if I could..." experimenter explains why she's had roughly fifteen careers and somehow survived them all with her sense of humour intact. Her work sits at the intersection of humans, pressure, and performance, drawing on experience across leadership, business, coaching, and high-stakes environments.

She's also a single mum of three (so yes, she has a PhD in "staying calm while someone loses a school hat five minutes before you need to leave"). With a bachelor of commerce, a master of science, and ongoing psychology training, Melinda is known for making nervous system science feel simple, practical, and oddly comforting.

She teaches one core truth: Calm isn't something you're born with—it's something you can learn.

You can find additional resources and contact Melinda directly at www.calmisaskill.com

www.ingramcontent.com/pod-product-compliance
Lightning Source LLC
LaVergne TN
LVHW010637110826
845149LV00014B/2862
9780987047977